With Kelly to Chitral

William George Laurence Beynon

Contents

CHAPTER I INTRODUCTORY 8
CHAPTER II THE MARCH BEGINS 11
CHAPTER III THE SHANDUR PASS 16
CHAPTER IV FROM LASPUR TO GASHT 28
CHAPTER V CHOKALWAT..35
CHAPTER VI THE RECONNAISSANCE FROM MASTUJ.............................43
CHAPTER VII THE FIGHT AT NISA GOL...52
CHAPTER VIII THE MARCH RESUMED THROUGH KILLA DRASAN..........61
CHAPTER IX NEARING CHITRAL 67
CHAPTER X WE REACH THE GOAL 74

WITH KELLY TO CHITRAL

BY

William George Laurence Beynon

GILGIT,
21st October 1895

MY DEAR MOTHER,
Before you read this short history of a few brief weeks, I must warn you that it is no record of exciting adventure or heroic deeds, but simply an account of the daily life of British officers and Indian troops on a frontier expedition.

How we lived and marched, what we ate and drank, our small jokes and trials, our marches through snow or rain, hot valleys or pleasant fields, in short, all that contributed to fill the twenty-four hours of the day is what I have to tell.

I write it for you, and that it may please you is all I ask.--Your son,

W.B.

CHAPTER I
INTRODUCTORY

"Would you like to go up to Gilgit?"

"Rather."

I was down in the military offices at Simla, hunting for a book and some maps, when I was asked the above question. No idea of Gilgit had before entered my head, but with the question came the answer, and I have since wondered why I never before thought of applying for the billet.

This was at the end of June 1894, and on the 24th August I was crossing the Burzil pass into the Gilgit district. As day broke on the 31st August, I dropped down several thousand feet from Doyen to Ramghat in the Indus valley, and it suddenly struck me I must have come down too low, and got into Dante's Inferno. As I passed under the crossbeam of the suspension bridge, I looked to find the motto, "All hope relinquish, ye who enter here." It wasn't there, but instead there was a sentry on the bridge, who, on being questioned, assured me that though there was not much to choose in the matter of temperature between the two places, I was still on the surface of the earth. He seemed an authority on the subject, so I felt happier, and accepted the cup of tea offered me by the commander of the guard.

Two hours later I was in Bunji, where I found I was to stay, and two days after that, an officer on his way down to Kashmir passed through, and almost the first question he asked me was, why on earth I had come up to Gilgit. "Gilgit's played out," said he. Well, I had been asked that question several times on my march up, so I may as well explain that there are officially two chief causes which send men up to Gilgit--one is debts, and the other, the Intelligence Branch. These, I say, are the official reasons, but the real reason is the chance of a "frontier row." In Simla they call them military expeditions. This accounts for the last part of that young officer's speech. There seemed no chance of a row to him, so he was going to other fields, and wondered at my coming up. At first, the result seemed to bear him out, as within two months he was on the war-path in Waziristan, while I was still kicking my heels at Bunji; but luck changed later, and I laughed last.

Well, to continue, my official reason for coming to Gilgit being the Intelligence Branch, I was ordered up to Chitral early in November for some survey work, and thus obtained the knowledge of the route and country that was to stand me in such good stead later on. I finished my work in Chitral in ten days, starting back for Gilgit on the 1st December, arriving there on the 19th. I spent Christmas in Gilgit, and started on the 2nd January 1895 for Hunza, where I expected to remain for the rest of the winter. News of the murder of Nizam-ul-mulk, Mehter of Chitral, reached Gilgit on the 7th January, and Dr. Robertson, Political Agent at Gilgit, at once made preparations for a visit to Chitral.

Captain Townshend, who was at Gupis with Gough of the 2nd Gurkhas, received orders to march with two hundred and fifty rifles of the 4th Kashmir Infantry. The first detachment started under Gough, the second following under Townshend The British Agent, Captain Campbell, and Surgeon Captain Whitchurch, joined the second party at Ghizr, and they all crossed the pass together. At Mastuj they picked up the remainder of the 14th Sikhs, under Harley, who had not gone down to Gurdon at Chitral, and then started for Chitral, arriving there on the 31st January. Lieutenant Moberly went from Gilgit with a detachment of the 4th Kashmir Infantry and took command of Mastuj. Gough returning to Ghizr, Baird took over command of Gupis, which was garrisoned by the 6th Kashmir Infantry, and I was brought down from Hunza to take over Baird's billet as staff officer. Shortly after, Fowler, R.E., was ordered to Chitral with his Bengal Sappers, and Edwardes, 2nd Bombay Infantry, to the same place, to take command of the Hunza Nagar Levies, which were now called out. Baird was next ordered up to Chitral and relieved by Stewart, R.A. On 21st February, Ross and Jones and the detachment of 14th Sikhs left Gilgit *en route* for Mastuj. The Hunza and Nagar Levies came in to Gilgit on the 7th March. I issued Snider carbines and twenty rounds ammunition to each man, and they left the next day. These Levies were splendid men, hardy, thick-set mountaineers, incapable of fatigue; and, as a distinguishing badge, each man was provided with a strip of red cloth which they wore in their caps, but which, we afterwards found by practical experience at Nisa Gol, was inadequate.

As news from Chitral had ceased for some days, Captain Stewart, Assistant British Agent in Gilgit, determined to call up the 32nd Pioneers, who were working on the Chilas road, so as to be ready for an advance in case any forward movement was necessary. In consequence of this order, Colonel Kelly marched into Gilgit on the 20th March with two hundred men, Borradaile following on the 22nd with a like party. On the 21st we heard from Mastuj that Ross's party of 14th Sikhs had been cut up, Ross himself and some forty-six Sepoys being killed, Jones and fourteen men alone managing to cut their way back; he and nine of the survivors being wounded. There was no news of Edwardes and Fowler. This news upset the apple-cart, and telegrams began to fly around, with the result that Colonel Kelly was put in command of the troops in the Gilgit district, with full civil powers on his line of operations. This telegram arrived on the evening of the 22nd. The day before, Colonel Kelly had offered me the position of staff officer to the force, and I naturally jumped at the chance. Dew of the Guides, who was on the sick-list, was sufficiently well to take over my work, so there was no difficulty on that score; and as I had long had my kit ready for any emergency, I merely bundled my remaining possessions into boxes, which I locked up and left to look after themselves till my return.

Here I may as well describe what the force consisted of. First, there were four hundred men of the 32nd Pioneers, commanded by Borradaile, Colonel Kelly having taken command of the column. Bar these two, we were all subalterns. Peterson was the senior, and commanded the second detachment, as we were marching to Ghizr in two parties. Then there was Bethune the adjutant, and Cobbe, and Browning-Smith the doctor--these were all 32nd Pioneers. Captain de Vismes, 10th Bombay Infantry, came along with us as far as Gupis, where he relieved Stewart, R.A., who, of course, was in command of the two guns of No. 1 Kashmir Mountain Battery. Stewart is an Irishman and the most bloodthirsty individual I have come across. He used to complain bitterly because the Chitralis wouldn't give us a fight every day. Then there was Luard, the Agency Surgeon; we used to chaff him considerably during the march to Gupis, as he turned up in a Norfolk jacket and a celluloid collar. I think he had sent his kit on to Gupis; at any rate, after that place he dressed in Khaki uniform like the rest of us. These were all who started from Gilgit, so I'll introduce the others as we pick them up.

CHAPTER II
THE MARCH BEGINS

Colonel Kelly assumed command on the 22nd March, and the next morning the first detachment of two hundred Pioneers, under Borradaile, marched off. The local Bible, commonly known as the Gazetteer, states that it never rains in Gilgit; this being so, it naturally started to rain on the morning of the 23rd, and kept it up for two days. We were marching without tents, so the first night the men had to run up their waterproof sheets into shelters.

Colonel Kelly, Luard, and myself started about 2 P.M. to catch up the troops, who had started about 9 A.M. Luard had a beast of a pulling pony, and as his double bridle hadn't got a curb chain, it was about as much use as a headache, so I suggested he should let the pony rip, and promised to bury his remains if he came a cropper. He took my advice and ripped; you couldn't see his pony's heels for dust as he disappeared across the plain. We found him all right in camp when we got there.

The men were already in camp, and pretty comfortable, in spite of the rain. Colonel Kelly had a small tent, and the rest of us turned into convenient cow-sheds. We were not troubled with much baggage, bedding, greatcoats, and a change of clothing; the men had poshteens (sheepskin coats), and everybody pleased themselves in the matter of boots, most of us preferring chuplies--a native kind of sandal with a leather sock, a very good article in snow, as you can put on any number of socks without stopping the circulation of blood in your feet. Officers and men were all provided with goggles, and very necessary they were.

We had a very jolly mess. The force being so small, the 32nd Pioneers kindly asked the remaining officers to mess with them, every man of course providing his own plate, knife, fork, and spoon, the cooking pots being collected for the general good. We had breakfast before starting, the hour for marching being 7 A.M. as a rule. The Pioneers had some most excellent bacon; good eggs and bacon will carry a man through a long day most successfully. I remember that when that bacon gave out, there was more mourning than over all the first-born of Egypt. Mutton we never ran out of; like the poor, it was always with us.

We got into camp as a rule some time in the afternoon, and then indulged in tea and chupatties; whisky was precious, and kept for dinner, which took place at dusk. Sometimes, when we got into camp late, dinner and tea were merged into one; however, it made no odds, we were always ready to eat when anything eatable came along. The mess provided some camp tables, and most of us managed to bring a camp stool, so we were in the height of luxury. After dinner a pipe or two, and then we turned in; we generally managed to get some grass to put under our blankets, but if we didn't, I don't think it made much difference; we were all young, and used to sleeping out on the hillside after game, frequently above the snow line, so it was no new experience. If it rained or was cold, we generally managed to get into a hut; these are remarkably strongly built, good stone walls, and thick, flat, wooden roofs with a mud covering, a hole in the middle of the floor for the fire, and a hole in the roof for the smoke--at least that was what we supposed was the idea, but the smoke generally preferred to remain inside.

There were also other discomforts of a minor nature. For instance, the cows and goats used to take it as a personal matter if you objected to their sharing the room with you; they were big enough, however, to catch and turn out, but there were other occupants of a more agile nature, armies of them, whom it was hopeless to try and eject; we suffered so much from their pleasing attentions that we generally preferred to sleep outside, weather permitting.

Our second march was to a village called Suigal in the Punyal district, governed by Raja Akbar Khan, a jolly old chap who came out to meet us on the road; he lives in a castle on the left bank of the river, which is here crossed by one of the highest and longest rope bridges in the country. In spite of his size, he is a very good polo player, as are all his family, some of whom were shut up in the Chitral Fort with Dr. Robertson. He now offered his services and those of his people to Government, which Colonel Kelly accepted, and the old man retired very pleased, to rejoin us later on. At Suigal we managed to get all the troops under shelter, as it was still raining, and it was now the second day that they had been wet through.

The next day the rain had luckily stopped, and towards noon the sun came out, and everybody's dampened spirits cheered up. We marched that day to Hoopar Pari, making a double march instead of halting at Gurkuch. Pari means a cliff--and the camping ground is a horrid little place shut in by high cliffs close to the bed of the river. There is no village near. It is a desolate place at the best of times, and when there is any wind blowing, it is like camping in a draught-pipe.

From Hoopar Pari we marched to Gupis. Gupis is a fort built by the Kashmir troops last year, on the most scientific principle, the only drawback being that it is commanded on all sides, and would be perfectly untenable if attacked by three men and a boy armed with accurate long-range rifles. Here we picked up Stewart, who was turning catherine wheels at the thought of taking his beloved guns into action. He expressed a desire to try a few shells on the neighbouring villages, to practise his men in ranging; but as there were objections to this plan, the idea was allowed to drop. At Gupis we made a raid on the stores in the officers' quarters and pretty well cleared them out. De Vismes, who took command, had to get a fresh supply up from Gilgit.

We had a merry dinner that night, provided, I think, by Stewart, who used to get up at intervals and dance a jig at the idea of seeing his guns the next morning--they were coming on with the second detachment under Peterson. From Gupis I sent my pony back to Gilgit, as it was useless taking it any farther, as we doubted being able to take animals over the pass, which eventually proved to be impossible. From Gupis onwards we had to be content with the usual hill track of these countries, good enough for a country pony, but still nothing to be proud of; here we discarded our Government mules, and took coolie transport instead. The march from Gupis to Dahimal is a long, trying one, up and down all the way. Cobbe, who was on rearguard, didn't get in till long after dark.

The village of Dahimal lies on the opposite bank of the river, so we did not cross, but bivouacked on the right bank, where there was some scrub jungle that provided us with wood. The Pioneers had brought four ducks; they were carried in a basket along with the mess-stores. Browning-Smith, who ran the messing, got quite pally with these ducks, and as soon as they were let out of their basket, he used to call them, and off they would waddle after him in search of a convenient puddle. I forget when those ducks were eaten, but I don't remember them at Ghizr, and am sure they didn't cross the pass.

Our next march was a short one to Pingal, only about nine miles. Here we were met by Mihrbhan Shah, the Hakim or governor of the upper part of the valley. Mihrbhan Shah is a bit of an authority in the murder line, having been employed by the late lamented Nizam-ul-mulk as chief murderer. Mihrbhan Shah is particularly proud of one of his little jobs, which he flatters himself he accomplished in a very neat and artistic manner. I forget the details, but it resulted in the death of five men. I asked him in to afternoon tea, Shah Mirza acting as interpreter. We had a long chat, from which I gained some very useful details about the state of the parties in Chitral, who was likely to help, and who wasn't, also a description of the road to Killa Drasan, which I did not know. This latter information seemed so important that I reported it that night to Colonel Kelly, and it was then and there decided to march *via* Killa Drasan instead of by the usual road through Buni.

I don't, think I have mentioned Shah Mirza before, so I will introduce him now, as he was one of our most useful allies, and is now one of my greatest friends. He belongs to the Punyal family, and is Wazir or governor of Sai and Gor. He lives at Damot, a village in the Sai valley, opposite Bunji, and it was during my stay there that I first got to know him. He has an interesting history, and, among other adventures, has travelled through the Pamirs and Chitral in disguise. He was our chief interpreter, and he, or one of his followers, of whom he had five, always kept near us. His followers were enlisted Levies, and one of them had formerly been my shikaree; in fact, he only left me as he was called out as a levy.

It is the custom of the country for the headmen of districts to come and pay their respects to any Sahib who may travel through their country, and the proper etiquette is to supply your visitors with tea and sweetmeats--biscuits will do just as well, and they like plenty of sugar. They then pay you the most barefaced compliments, and make the startling assertion that you are their father and mother; upon which you reply that all you have is at their disposal. If they have any petition,--and they generally have,--they insinuate it gently in the general conversation, so you have to be looking out for traps of this sort. When you have suffered sufficient evil for the day, you mildly suggest that they are probably fatigued, and would like to rest. They take the hint, and the remainder of the biscuits, and depart. We used to have lots of these visits, which went by the name of "political teas."

Mihrbhan Shah proved very useful to us, I fancy he knew he would get small mercy if he fell into the hands of the opposition, and therefore did all he could to place our force between them and himself. Both at Pingal and our next halting place, Cheshi, he managed to billet all our small force in the villages, and no doubt our men were very thankful as we were getting pretty high up, and the nights were decidedly cold. Although it was a friendly district, we had regular pickets and sentries, and a British officer on duty to see everything was correct.

CHAPTER III
THE SHANDUR PASS

Shortly after leaving Pingal, the character of the country changed considerably, and instead of a continual alternation of cliff and river bed, the valley became more open and level; we were, in fact, nearing the upper end of the valley. Beyond Cheshi the road leads up a bluff and down the other side on to the bed of the Pandur Lake. This lake had, at the beginning of 1894, been a sheet of water some four and a half miles long, but, the dam at its end having given way in July, it had drained off rapidly; and when I had crossed it in November of the same year, the mud of its bed was only just becoming firm and was cracked and fissured in every direction. It was now covered with a sheet of snow, through which the river twined dark and muddy.

We had now reached the snow line, and our green goggles were taken into use. The march of our column churned the snow and mud into a greasy slime, and the going was very tiring. However, we came in sight of the Ghizr post by 2 P.M., and Gough, of the 2nd Gurkhas, who was in command, came out to meet us. From him we learned that none of his messengers that had been sent to Mastuj with letters had returned, and it was now some ten days since the last communication had reached him; so it became evident that the enemy were between Laspur and Mastuj. We knew that they had not crossed the pass, or we should have seen them before this, so we were pretty hopeful of a fight soon after crossing the pass, and we were not disappointed. At Ghizr we also found Oldham, a Sapper subaltern, who had preceded us by a few days. He had with him a party of Kashmir Sappers and Miners, who were now armed with Snider carbines. The post, which consisted of a block of isolated houses, had been fortified and surrounded with a thorn zareba, and was only sufficiently large for the garrison of Kashmir troops then holding it, so our men were billeted in the neighbouring houses, one of which we turned into a mess and quarters for ourselves.

We halted on the 30th March, in order to allow the second detachment of the Pioneers and the guns to come up, as from here Colonel Kelly intended to march in one column. Here also we picked up the Hunza and Nagar Levies, numbering a hundred men, under their own leaders. They were posted in the village of Teru, some four miles up the valley, and from there could give timely warning if any hostile force crossed the pass. Wazir Humayun led the Hunza crowd, and Wazir Taifu the Nagar. I got to know Humayun very well indeed, and a right good sort he is. He had formerly lived for some five years in Chitral, when Raja Safdar Ali Khan of Hunza had made things too hot for him, but when Safdar Ali fled when we took the country in 1891-92, he was reinstated. Wazir Taifu I did not get to know so well, as the Nagar Levies were left behind at Mastuj, when we went on from there to Chitral. The second detachment under Peterson, and the guns with Stewart, got into camp some time after midday on the 31st March.

In the meantime, every available coolie and pony had been collected, and we calculated on being able to start the next morning, with ten days' rations for the whole force. By 6 A.M. on the 1st April the troops had fallen in and were ready to start, and a nice handy little lot we had. Four hundred Pioneers, two mountain guns, forty Kashmir Sappers and a hundred Levies. Then the coolies were told to load up, and the trouble began. It now appeared that some hundred coolies and ponies from Yasin had bolted during the night. We had put too much faith in Mihrbhan Shah's influence, and all those villagers who were not directly under his government had gone. Those hundred coolies meant the transport of our supplies, and without them we should only have the food actually carried in the men's haversacks. We had cut down our baggage to the vanishing point, and the men were carrying all they could, and we did not dare leave our reserve ammunition behind.

The column had just moved off when this state of things became known and was reported to me. Colonel Kelly was at the head of the column, so I snatched the nearest pony, tumbled its load on to the ground, and went scrambling through the snow after the troops. Of course there was nothing to be done except halt the column until the coolies could be collared and brought back, so Stewart, who had a battery pony with him, was sent off down the road after the absconding coolies.

They must have started the evening before, as he only caught a few of them up fifteen miles back, and had great difficulty in bringing them along with him. We met him as we were returning to Ghizr at seven o'clock that evening. Stewart had scarcely gone ten minutes before some fifty coolies were found hiding in a village; they were soon driven out and made to lift their loads. This gave us some six days' rations, and with it we moved off, our great object being to get across the pass and open communications with Mastuj. After that we could see about getting on to Chitral. Our transport consisted of country ponies and coolies, and I remained behind to see the last off and rearguard moving before I started myself.

About two miles from Ghizr post there was a steep ascent where the road twisted and curled among a mass of debris fallen from the cliffs above, and in one place the ponies had to be helped through a narrow passage between two fallen boulders. About midday I caught up the tail of the troops, who were already past the village of Teru, the highest inhabited spot in the valley; there are only a few houses, and these are scattered about in clumps a few hundred yards apart. Passing on, I caught up the battery, and reached the leading infantry, when suddenly the word to halt was passed down the long line.

We were now on a narrow plain, and the snow on either hand of the track which the troops were following in single file was over my waist, as I soon found whenever I left the path in order to reach more quickly the head of the column. On arriving there, I found the track had suddenly ended, and before us was the level expanse of snow-covered valley. Attempts were being made to get the gun mules of the battery through this, but at every step they sank up to their girths, even then not finding firm foothold. Trials were then made of the ground at the sides of the valley, but the snow was found equally deep and soft there; and after spending an hour or so in futile attempts to get forward, it became evident to all that no animal could possibly pass over the snowfield in its present condition. We had only gone some eight miles out of the thirteen to Langar, and it was already three o'clock. There was nothing, therefore, for it but to return, and the word to retire was reluctantly passed along the line, and each man, turning where he stood, moved slowly back towards Ghizr.

But though laden or unladen animals could not cross the pass, we saw no reason to suppose that men could not, and therefore, at Teru, which we reached by four o'clock, a halt was made, and two hundred Pioneers, with Borradaile and Cobbe, and the Sappers under Oldham, were detailed to remain there with the Hunza Levies, and to try and force their way across the pass the next day. Borradaile was to receive all the coolie transport, which he was to send back as soon as he got across the pass, in order that we might follow with the remainder of the troops. His orders were to entrench himself at Laspur, which was the first village across the pass, and if possible open communications with Mastuj.

The guns were immediately sent back to Ghizr, and we set to work to sort out the kits of Borradaile's party from the remainder. The unavoidable confusion at first was something dreadful. First of all, the kits had to be unloaded, then those of Borradaile's party separated and put on one side; the remaining kits were then loaded on the ponies and sent off, as fast as the ponies could be loaded up, back to Ghizr. The ammunition had to be divided, and as much as possible given over in the way of supplies. All this time we had to have a ring of sentries round to stop the coolies from bolting, but as soon as we had got the ponies off, the coolies were collected, and sat down in the snow under a guard. Borradaile's party were then told off into the different houses, and the coolies likewise, still under guard, the ammunition and supplies stacked, and the job was done.

By this time it was about seven o'clock, getting dark, and also beginning to snow. All of us, officers and men, were covered with slush and mud from head to foot, and dripping wet. Smith, who was going with Borradaile's party, had, however, managed to get a fire going in one of the houses, and had got some tea ready, bless him! We had a cup all round, and wished Borradaile and his party good luck. The remainder of us plunged out into the darkness and snow and splashed back to Ghizr. The men, who had started some time before us, were comfortably in their former quarters when we reached Ghizr.

On the way we met Stewart, who had just returned from his coolie hunt, and was seated on a rock, like Rachel mourning for her children, only in his case he was murmuring, not because the guns were not, but because they were back in Ghizr. "His guns were going over that pass even if he had to carry them himself, you may bet your boots on that! and begad, I'll set the gunners to cut a road; and d'ye think now the snow would bear the mules at night when it was frozen at all?"

We got back to the huts we had left in the morning by 8.30 P.M., and there was a general demand for something hot. Our servants, luckily, had been sent back straight, so it was not long before we had something to eat; that was our first meal since 5.30 A.M., and it was now about 9 P.M. We had marched some sixteen miles through snow, and been on foot for some fifteen hours, and here we were back in the same place we had started from. Since midday we had been pretty well wet through, and the wind and cold had peeled the skin off our faces till it hung in flakes; still we were lucky in having a roof over our heads, as it had now started to snow in earnest. After dinner we weren't long before turning in.

We were up early the next morning, but Stewart and Gough were up still earlier, and were making sledges and trying experiments with loads. They came in flushed with success, swearing that they had dragged the whole ammunition of the guns by themselves across half a mile of snow, and that they would have the guns over the pass in no time. Unluckily, the snow was still falling, and as Borradaile had all the available coolie transport, we were forced to wait till he could send it back. By noon he sent in a letter by one of the levies, saying he had been unable to start, as heavy snow was still falling, but would try the next day.

Shah Mirza now came up to me and said that there was a mullah in the village who had an infallible charm for stopping the snow, and a present of a few rupees would no doubt set it in motion. I promptly inquired how it was the mullah was not carrying a load, but was told he was too old to help in that way, but would be only too delighted to overcome the elements; so I gave the Mirza to understand that if the mullah would stop the snow-storm the Sirkar would make him, the mullah, a great man; in the meantime, I would give him a couple of rupees on account. Shah Mirza went off joyfully, evidently having implicit faith in the mullah.

Shortly after this, Gough came up, saying that the Kashmir troops in the post had volunteered to make a road through the snow, and if he could take fifty of them with four days' rations to Teru, a sufficient track might be made to Langar, our next camping ground, just this side of the pass, to enable the guns to be carried there without much difficulty. Colonel Kelly's permission having been obtained, we set about collecting all the shovels and spades we could find in the village. Among others I got hold of the mullah's, who became very indignant; but I pointed out to him that as his prayers seemed to have no effect on the snow, perhaps his shovel would make up for their deficiencies. We managed, by instituting a house-to-house visitation, to collect some twenty spades of sorts, and with those supplied by the troops, we got altogether some forty, which were handed over to Gough. He and Stewart and fifty Kashmir Sepoys started off that day to Teru, taking with them half a dozen sledges that had been made out of ghi boxes.

Later in the day we had to send out foraging parties for wood and bhoosa (chopped straw) as the commissariat reported their supply as running out; in fact, these parties had to go out every day during our stay in Ghizr.

Early the next morning I got a note from Stewart, asking that the battery might be sent up to Teru, as there was enough fodder there for the mules, and experiments could be made for getting the guns along. I got the battery off sharp, but it was nearly noon before they got to Teru. The snow had ceased falling, and, the clouds clearing off, the sun made a blinding glare off the freshly fallen snow.

After breakfast I started off for Teru myself, to see how Borradaile was getting along, and, finding he had started, I left my borrowed pony at the village, and, pushing on, caught up the rearguard a short way beyond where we had been forced to turn back on the 1st April. Here I found Stewart, Gough, and Oldham with the fifty Kashmir troops, two Sappers and Miners, and rearguard of the Pioneers, staggering along under the guns and ammunition in a track that had been beaten out by the troops marching in front. For some reason or other the sledges did not seem to act, partly, I think, because the track, being made by men marching in single file, was too narrow and uneven; at anyrate, when I arrived, the guns, wheels, carriages, and ammunition had been told off to different squads, about four men carrying the load at a time, and being relieved by a fresh lot every fifty yards or so. Even thus the rate of progression was fearfully slow, about one mile an hour, and the men were continually sinking up to their waists in snow. Added to this, there was a bitter wind, and a blinding glare, while the men were streaming with perspiration.

I know my own face felt as if it had been dipped in boiling water, and during the next few days the whole skin came off in flakes.

I may as well here describe the tribulations of the advanced party, prefacing my remarks by saying that they are founded on reports and hearsay, and therefore I beg any slight inaccuracy may be forgiven me. When I turned back to return to Ghizr, the party carrying the guns were just arriving at a stream called the Shamalkhand, which flows from a high pass of the same name, which is often used as a summer route to Mastuj, but at that time of year is impassable. From this stream to Langar, the camping ground on the eastern side of the Shandur Pass, is some four miles, the valley being open and fairly level, but covered with thick dwarf willow on the banks of the stream flowing down the centre which confines the road to the western side of the valley. The main body of the party I could see about one and a half miles ahead; they had already crossed the stream. That was about 4 P.M., and the rearguard did not get into camp till 11 P.M., and even then the guns had to be left about a mile from camp.

At Langar there is only one little wretched hut about six feet square, which was used as a shelter by the officers and one or two sick men, the remainder huddling round fires in the snow. Luckily, as I have already said, there was a plentiful supply of wood to be had for the cutting. Many of the men, I hear, were too tired to cook their food, but simply lay down exhausted near the fires, the officers getting something to eat about midnight. Very little sleep was there for either officers or men that night, most of them passed it huddled up round the fires, or stamping up and down to keep warm.

Early the next morning the Pioneers and Levies started to cross the pass, while the remainder brought the guns into camp, which work, I believe, took the best part of the day.

On leaving the camping ground, the track leads sharply to the right, following the course of the Shandur stream, which is now merely a rushing brook. The ascent is fairly precipitous for about a mile, and is followed by a very gradual ascent,--so gradual, in fact, that it is difficult to say when the top of the pass is actually reached. This slope constitutes the pass, and is some five miles long, and twelve thousand three hundred and twenty feet above the sea; absolutely bare of trees, and with two fair-sized lakes upon its surface, it is easy to imagine the deadly cold winds that sweep across it. The lakes were now frozen over, and the valley was one even sheet of spotless snow lying dazzling under the sun. It is this combination of sun and snow which causes so much discomfort and snow blindness; I had before crossed this same pass in December on a cloudy day, and although the whole of it was covered with freshly fallen snow, I did not even find it necessary to wear the goggles I had in my pocket ready for use.

The distance from Langar on the east to the village of Laspur on the west of the pass is not more than ten miles, yet Borradaile's party, leaving Langar at daybreak, did not reach Laspur till seven o'clock at night.

Strange as it may seem, the men suffered greatly from thirst, and from some mistaken idea of becoming violently ill if they did so, they refused to eat the snow through which they were floundering. Towards evening, as they reached the western end of the pass, three men, evidently an outpost of the enemy, were seen to bolt from behind some rocks and make good their escape, in spite of an attempt by the Levies to catch them.

The descent from the pass to the village of Laspur is some two miles long, and down a steep and rather narrow ravine. The Hunza Levies covered the spurs on each side, while the Pioneers descended down the centre. So sudden and unexpected was their arrival that the inhabitants were caught in the village, and naturally expressed their extreme delight at this unexpected visit--so polite of them, wasn't it? They also said that they would be glad to help us in any way we desired. They were taken at their word, and sent back next day to bring on the guns, while that night they were politely requested to clear out of some of their houses, which were quickly put into a state of defence and occupied by our troops. Supplies were also required of the village.

The next day was spent by the detachment in completing the defences, and collecting supplies and coolies. Towards evening a report was brought in that the enemy had collected to the number of about a hundred some three miles away. So Borradaile took out some of the men to reconnoitre. Some men were seen in the distance, but these the Levies declared to be only villagers, and as it was getting dusk, the party returned to camp, only then learning that a levy had been taken prisoner. The man had gone some distance ahead of his fellows, and had been captured by two men who jumped out on him from behind a rock. That evening the guns were brought in by the Kashmir troops and the coolies, amid cheers from the Pioneers.

Nothing, I think, can be said too highly in praise of this splendid achievement. Here were some two hundred and fifty men, Hindus and Mussulmans, who, working shoulder to shoulder, had brought two mountain guns, with their carriages and supply of ammunition, across some twenty miles of deep, soft snow, across a pass some twelve thousand three hundred and twenty feet high, at the beginning of April, the worst time of the year. It must also be remembered that these men were carrying also their own rifles, greatcoats, and eighty rounds of ammunition, and wearing heavy sheepskin coats; they had slept for two nights in the snow, and struggled from dawn till dark, sinking at every step up to their waists, and suffering acutely from a blinding glare and a bitter wind. So much for the rank and file; but in their officers they had had splendid examples to follow, especially Stewart and Gough, if one may select when all did so nobly. Both these officers took their turns with the men, Stewart with his gunners, and Gough with his Gurkhas, in carrying the guns, and both, with utter unselfishness and with complete disregard for their own personal comfort, gave their snow glasses to sepoys who, not having any, were suffering from the glare experienced on the first day. It is by these small acts that officers can endear themselves to their men, who, knowing that their officers have their welfare at heart, will follow wherever they may lead.

Thus was the Shandur Pass first crossed, and a position established from whence the force could work down to Mastuj and thence to Chitral.

I may here mention that so little did the Chitralis imagine that we could cross the pass, that letters were found in Laspur stating that the British force was lying in Ghizr, the men unable to move from frostbite, and the officers from snow blindness; also that since then fresh snow had fallen, and no forces would now be able to cross for several weeks. In fact, the Chitralis looked upon the game as entirely in their own hands; the surprise of our arrival was therefore all the more complete.

Having brought the guns and Borradaile's party safely across the pass, I return and relate Colonel Kelly's and my own experiences.

After leaving the guns being dragged through the snow to Langar on the 3rd April, I walked back to Teru. On the way I saw the mullah's shovel sticking up in the snow, with one half of the blade snapped off. Alas, poor mullah! At Teru I found the battery mules and drivers; these were ordered back to Ghizr, as they could be more easily fed there, and would be protected by the garrison of the post. I eventually got back to Ghizr before dark and reported events, and, just my luck, got a bad go of fever the next day. Great Scott! I did feel a worm! I was shivering with ague and my face was like a furnace. I hadn't a bit of skin on it either, and it was painful to eat or laugh from the cracked state of my lips. I managed to struggle through some necessary official letters, but as a staff officer that day I was not much use.

Colonel Kelly determined to start himself the next morning, with the Nagar Levies and Shah Mirza, as we had managed to collect half a dozen coolies to carry our kits. I went with Colonel Kelly, the remainder of the Pioneers coming on as soon as the coolies from Borradaile's party arrived; we were expecting them the next day, the 5th April.

I turned in early that night, after having covered my raw face with some Vinolia powder that Colonel Kelly happened to have. I had not before known that these powders were supposed to be of any use. I had a vague sort of idea that they were used for sprinkling babies, but was unaware of the reason of this strange rite; however, I will now give the Vinolia Company what I believe is called an unsolicited testimonial. I stuck to that powder till I got to Mastuj, by which time my face had become human again. Colonel Kelly had a beard, so he didn't suffer so much. The next morning I felt much better, had no fever, and, thanks to the Vinolia, my face was much less painful.

We got the Levies and our kits off early, and about noon Colonel Kelly and I started on some borrowed ponies, which we rode as far as we could and then sent back. Having caught up the Levies, we tramped forward along the track made by the first column, occasionally finding deserted sledges and bits of broken spades. The snow was now somewhat firmer than when the first party had crossed, owing to the top of the snow thawing slightly in the sun every day and being frozen hard again every night; all the same, the slightest divergence from the track plunged us up to our waists in snow.

The only one of our party who could walk on the snow without difficulty was my bull-terrier "Bill," a spotted dog of doubtful ancestry. He had been given to me as a bull-terrier when he was only a little white rat of a thing, and I had raised him at Bunji on tinned milk. He was a most uncanny dog (the joke is unintentional), and it was commonly believed in the force that his father was a tom cat. Poor Bill! Before he got to Laspur he was so snow blind that until we got to Mastuj I had to open his eyes for him every morning and bathe them with hot water before he could see, and he was hardly well again a month later.

We got into camp that night before dusk, pretty well fagged and wet, and as soon as the coolies came in with our kits, we scraped a hole in the snow and pitched the colonel's small tent. In camp we found a few men who had been placed in charge of some ammunition that had been left behind for want of transport. This guard were mostly suffering a bit from snow blindness, but were otherwise all right, as they had run up shelters and had plenty of wood and their bedding. When I got at my kit, I took out a bottle of quinine and dosed our servants and orderlies all round, so that they should not have any excuse for getting fever, and then took some myself for the same reason. We then laid out our bedding in the tent, while the servants went into the hut, and turned in immediately after dinner, and had a very comfortable night.

We were up before dawn the next morning, and, as we had slept in our clothes, it was not long before we had had breakfast and struck camp. By 6 A.M. we were climbing the ascent to the pass. There was a wind whistling straight in our faces, and I had no idea anything could be so cold; it simply went clean through you, and I quite expected to hear my ribs sing like an Aeolian harp. When we got on to the pass, the sun rose and the wind dropped quite suddenly, and presently we had taken off our greatcoats on account of the heat. After going about an hour, I began to suffer from mountain sickness, a curious and distinctly unpleasant sensation, very much like having a rope tied tightly round one's chest and back, and the shortness of breath necessitating a halt every hundred yards or so. Colonel Kelly did not suffer from it at all, but trudged along without a halt the whole way. That is the only time I have ever suffered from mountain sickness, and I have crossed the Shandur both before and since, as also other passes, without feeling any inconvenience.

By noon we had almost reached the highest point of the pass, and were skirting the larger lake, when we met the coolies of Borradaile's party returning with an escort of some of the Kashmir troops. They all seemed pretty lively in spite of the poor time they had been having; but as they are used to crossing the Shandur at all times of the year, I daresay our sympathy was a good deal wasted.

We were soon descending into the Laspur valley, and we had hardly dropped three hundred feet before all sense of sickness left me, and I felt as fit as possible. A short way out of the village we were met by a patrol which Borradaile had sent out to meet us, and by two o'clock we were in camp, where we found Oldham in command, Borradaile having gone on a reconnaissance down the valley. The previous day news had been brought in that the enemy were assembled in the valley, and a small party had gone out, as I have already related. On the morning of the 6th April,

Borradaile accordingly determined on another reconnaissance, this time taking the guns with him, they being carried by Laspuri villagers, who no doubt thought the game very poor fun. Gough went with the party, Oldham remaining in command of the post, which was garrisoned with the maimed, the halt, and the blind--in other words, with men suffering from frostbite and snow blindness, of whom there were some twenty-six of the former and thirty of the latter; those men of the Kashmir troops who were fit to march being sent back across the pass as escort to the coolies.

When the reconnoitring party had gone some three miles down the valley, they came across the old camp fires of the enemy. At Rahman, two miles farther on, they left the snow behind, much to everybody's delight, and by one o'clock entered the village of Gasht, some eleven miles from Laspur, and about half-way to Mastuj, the Levies crowning a small knoll in the middle of the valley at the lower end of the village. From here they reported they could see the enemy some three miles farther down the valley, who were evidently engaged in building sangars and entrenching themselves. A short council of war was held as to the advisability of attacking them, but, considering that the force consisted of only a little over a hundred men and some fifty Levies, besides the two guns, and also the time of day, it was decided to return to camp, which was reached by dark. The day's work was highly creditable to all concerned; the march to Gasht and back had been some twenty-two miles, and information had been obtained of the position in which we might expect opposition from the enemy. On getting into camp, Borradaile's party found Colonel Kelly and myself waiting their arrival, eager to hear their news.

CHAPTER IV
FROM LASPUR TO GASHT

That night we had beef for dinner. This may appear a trivial fact, but it meant a great and blessed change from the eternal mutton we had been living on, none of us having tasted beef for quite six months, except in its condensed or tinned state, which does not count. Gilgit is a dependency of Kashmir, whose ruling family, being Hindus, strongly object to cow-killing, and therefore the law runs that no cows are to be slaughtered; hence none of us since crossing the bridge at Kohalla had tasted fresh beef. But now we were in Chitral territory, and a Mussulman country, so we were free to kill cows, but did so unostentatiously, as nearly all our force were Hindus. The dark deed was accomplished thus: on the houses being searched on the arrival of the first party at Laspur, an innocent little calf was found in one of the houses, and quick as thought then and there despatched. I will not reveal the murderer's name, because I do not know it. All traces were removed, and for the next few days we enjoyed hot roast beef.

We were a merry party, but what a set of ruffians we looked! Stewart and Gough were both suffering from snow blindness, owing to their generous action in giving their goggles to sepoys, and passed most of their spare time with their heads over a basin of hot water, dabbing their aching eyes; none of us had much skin on our faces, and what little remained was of a patchwork description; none of us had shaved for days--we couldn't have stood the torture; and our clothes, too, were showing signs of wear and tear. We all now slept in our clothes, partly for the sake of warmth, and also to be in readiness in case of emergency. There we were, sitting or lying on our bedding, which was spread on the floor round the room, the latter divided, like all Chitrali houses, into loose stalls by low partitions, a small fire burning in the centre of the room, from which a thick pillar of smoke rose and hung like a cloud from the roof, through a hole in which part of it escaped. Our swords and revolvers were hanging on the walls or from pegs in the beams, the whole scene dimly lit by one or two candles. It might look very picturesque, but I always consider the best hotel is good enough for me.

As there was not space enough in the stalls for all of us, Colonel Kelly and I, as the last comers, slept in a little room off the main one; here was evidently the winter store of fodder for the cattle as it was half full of bhoosa (chopped straw). This we spread evenly over the floor to the depth of some two feet, and then laid our blankets on top. There was just room enough for us to lie out straight, the Colonel taking one side and I the other, and a softer or more luxurious bed could hardly be imagined. We had to be careful, though, not to drop matches about, and to put out our pipes before going to sleep. A halt had been ordered for the following day, to give the men suffering from snow blindness and frostbite a chance to recover, so we turned in with the blissful consciousness of not having to turn out at dawn, and slept like the dead.

The next day, April 7, was spent in hurrying forward all arrangements for an advance on the morrow. We also sent round messengers to all the villagers to come in and make their submission, on pain of having their villages burned; and seeing that we now had the upper hand, at any rate in their valley, the inhabitants came in without much hesitation, and also brought in a certain amount of supplies; consequently by night we had sufficient local coolies to carry all our baggage, supplies, ammunition, and, most important of all, the two guns. About noon on this day, Raja Akbar Khan of Punyal, whom I have before mentioned as meeting us on the march from Shoroh to Suigal, came into camp with fifty Levies, bringing in a convoy of ninety Balti coolies with supplies. We were getting along famously now, so Colonel Kelly decided to advance the next day without waiting for Peterson's detachment, as our first object was to open communication with Mastuj.

We had a political tea that afternoon: all the leaders of the Levies, old Raja Akbar Khan, Humayun, Taifu, the Nagar Wazir, Shah Mirza, and one or two princelings who had come up to see some fighting, all squatted round our little room on the straw, swigging sweet tea and munching biscuits, quite a friendly gathering; in fact, so much tea was consumed that the mess president swore he would send in a bill.

We always got our earliest and most reliable information from the Levies, as most of them had blood relations among the Chitralis. They also knew just where to look for hidden grain and supplies of all sorts. As a rule there was generally a cache under or near the fireplace in the main room, but I have also seen the Levies find them in the most unlikely places, and very queer odds and ends they sometimes pulled out of these under-ground storerooms.

On the morning of April 8th the column was formed up and ready to start by 9 A.M. Poor Gough was being left behind at Laspur in command of the garrison, which consisted of some twenty-five Kashmir troops, and the Nagar and Punyal Levies, in all about a hundred. The Levies were to come on as soon as the second party arrived. Our force, therefore, consisted of two hundred Pioneers, two guns, forty Kashmir Sappers, and fifty Hunza Levies. Our order of march was as follows: first of all went the Levies; then, with an interval of some five hundred yards, came the advance guard of a half company of Pioneers; the main body consisted of Kashmir Sappers, guns, one company of Pioneers, ammunition, hospital baggage, and rear-guard of half company Pioneers. Both advance and rear-guards were commanded by British officers. It was a lovely, fine morning, and we were all in the best of spirits, and looking forward to leaving behind the detestable snow, and therewith our chief source of discomfort.

Poor old Gough looked awfully dismal at being left behind, but it was the fortune of war. At Gurkuch, at Gupis, at Ghizr, there was only one cry from officers and men--British and Native--"For Heaven's sake take us on with you!" The natives always added that they would never be able to face their womenfolk again if there had been fighting and they not in it. The Britisher expressed his disgust at what he called "his bally luck" in more forcible terms, but it meant the same thing, and we are all the same colour under the skin.

Off we went, through the village and across the stream by a rickety bridge, then down the left bank for about a mile, when we came to a small hamlet,--I forget its name,--and here I fell out and paid a visit to the house of Mahomed Rafi, the Hakim of the Laspur district. This hoary-headed old rascal had been playing fast and loose for a long time, but had at last cast in his lot openly with the enemy; he had a long list of offences to answer for, and is believed to be one of the actual murderers of Hayward about 1872.

Hayward was globe-trotting up Yasin way when these ruffians rushed his camp, seized him, and carried him into a wood with the intention of killing him. He asked them to defer the performance until daylight, as he should like to look on the world once more. This they agreed to, and soon after dawn made him kneel down and hacked off his head. Such is the story. Poor Hayward's body was brought into Gilgit, and he lies in an orchard close to the British Agency. I can quite imagine Hayward, or any man who has any appreciation of the grandeur of Nature in her wilder moods, wishing to see the sun rise once again over these tumbled masses of snow peaks and bare cliffs. The startling sensation of the immensity of these hills in comparison with man's minuteness strikes home with almost the stunning effect of a sudden blow.

It is said that the calm pluck of Hayward touched even his murderers, callous as they are to bloodshed It makes a sensational picture: a solitary figure in the foreground standing alone on the edge of a pine wood high up in the lonely grandeur of the everlasting hills, the first flush of dawn reddening the snow on peak after peak, changing the pure white to pink, the cold blue to purple, the tumbled sea of mountain summits gradually growing in distinctness, the soft mist rising from the valleys, and the group of wild figures standing within the shade of the pines. Hayward takes one long look on all this loveliness, and turns towards his executioners--men say that even they hesitated.

Mahomed Rafi, who was supposed to have actually killed Hayward, was now Hakim of Laspur, and, as I have said, had joined the enemy.

When I had travelled through Laspur in November last, the old ruffian had come to pay his respects, and accompanied me part of the way to Mastuj, and while doing so, had stopped at a house to give some orders, and had informed me that this was one of his houses. On passing it now, I thought a visit might be useful, so, getting Shah Mirza and his Levies, I got permission to search the house. It had evidently only recently been occupied for on bursting in the door we found the cooking pots in the fireplace and fresh meat hanging in one of the rooms. After a short search we found the grain store, with several mounds of grain, which was afterwards taken into Laspur. There was nothing much more that we could find in our hasty search, but I picked up an empty spectacle-case, astonished at finding it in such a place, as Mahomed Rafi never wore spectacles in his life. I showed it to Colonel Kelly, who promptly annexed it, as he was in want of one, having mislaid his own. Shah Mirza also collared a fowl, which no doubt formed his next meal.

I caught up the column before they had gone much more than a mile, just as they were crossing a stream. After that we had some level marching into the village of Rahman, and by this time the snow was only lying in patches. Here we made a short halt. From Rahman there is a path across the hills to Chitral, by means of a nullah called the Goland Gol, of which mention will be made hereafter but at this time of year it was impossible to use this path, owing to the snow.

During the halt, the headman of the village came up to make his salaams, and also told me that a man of Ghizr had passed through that morning, escaping from the enemy. He was reported to be one of Gough's messengers, captured when taking letters to Moberly at Mastuj. I told the headman that he had better show his goodwill by bringing in the man, which he promised to do, and sent him in that night to our camp at Gasht. We learned little from him, except that the enemy were going to fight us between Gasht and Mastuj, and that the latter place was all right. This man had no idea of numbers, and when asked the strength of the enemy, replied invariably that there were very many men, but seemed equally uncertain if there were five hundred or five thousand collected in the sangar before us, and yet he had been a prisoner in their camp for some fifteen days.

I found the best way of getting information out of the prisoners was to set Shah Mirza or Humayun on the job. They used to squat down over the fire with the prisoners and engage them in conversation gradually getting what they knew out of them by simple-looking questions. Of course I couldn't do this as I didn't know their language, and the presence of a British officer put them on their guard at once.

Between Rahman and Mastuj the country is pretty much the same, a narrow valley running between high, stony hills, their tops covered with snow and their feet with boulders; then the bed of the valley more or less rocky, and the river winding from side to side, and below the main level of the valley, at depths varying from fifty to two hundred feet, the sides nearly always sheer cliff; at intervals were nullahs, down which ran streams of snow water from the hills to the river, or fans of alluvial deposit brought down by floods in previous years. On the flank of one such fan we found the village of Gasht, which we reached by 3.30 P.M. The Levies had already occupied the knoll at the lower end of the village from whence the enemy had before been seen; so, after fixing on a camping ground and giving the necessary orders, the officers all went forward to have a look.

From the top of the knoll there was an extended view of the valley, and I was able to point out the position of Mastuj, which was hidden by some rising ground, and also the general direction of the road. About three miles ahead we could distinctly see a sangar filled with men on the left bank of the river. That sangar was, as far as we could judge, on the right flank of the enemy's line. A few men could also be seen climbing a steep stone shoot on the right bank of the river, so evidently the enemy were going to try the effect of a stone avalanche as we went underneath. A good deal of discussion went on as to whether the enemy's main defence was on the left bank, in which case we should have to attack across the river, or on the right bank, in which case the present visible sangar was a flanking bastion.

At last someone suggested tea, so the meeting broke up. Colonel Kelly and I stayed behind. I asked Colonel Kelly for permission to take some of the Levies and have a cast forward. I took the Hunza men and my shikaree, Faquir, as he could translate my orders to the Levies. Off we trotted, and by the time the other officers were having tea, I was well up the hillside. It was impossible to be rushed, as the ground was pretty bad, so I extended my men,--when it comes to sniping, one man is a smaller target than two,--and we skirmished up and forward, so as to bring us well above the enemy's line. In half an hour we were high enough to see all the valley below, and the enemy's position was spread out like a map. I sent the Levies on about a hundred yards, and then made them line a ridge, while I sat myself comfortably down and sketched the whole show.

With my glasses I could count the men in each sangar. They were evidently cooking their evening meal, as thin columns of smoke rose from each sangar in the still evening air. I could also make out the paths leading up the cliffs from the river, and saw men going down to fetch water. I sat and watched long after I had got all the information I wanted, as I might perhaps get some useful tips that I had overlooked. It was very peaceful sitting there, but presently the sun dropped behind the hills, and it got too chilly for comfort. A whistle to the Levies and a wave of the hand brought them back, and we scrambled down the hill again, and were back in camp before dark. Here I heard that the Punyal Levies had been sent for from

Laspur to come along at once.

As soon as I had explained the enemy's position to Colonel Kelly, orders were issued for the attack next day. They were short and simple. On the arrival of the Punyal Levies, they were to start, with a guide we had procured, to turn out the men above the stone shoot on the right bank of the river. I, with the Hunza Levies, was to start at 6 A.M. and work through the hills to the right rear of the enemy's position. The main body would start at 9 A.M. and attack in front. The baggage to remain in camp under a guard commanded by Sergt. Reeves, Commissariat. Then we had dinner and went to bed.

CHAPTER V
CHOKALWAT

At 5 A.M. the next morning, my orderly, Gammer Sing Gurung, woke me. It was still dark, and I dressed as quickly as possible, so as not to disturb the others, who were snoring peacefully around me. Dressing consisted of putting on my coat, putties, and some canvas shoes with rope soles. I knew the ground I should be going over would be pretty bad, and with rope soles you can skip about rocks like a young lamb, whereas shooting boots would send you flying over the cliffs. By the time I had had some poached eggs and a cup of tea, the Hunza Levies were waiting outside, so I got into my sword and trappings and went. As I passed out, Colonel Kelly wished me good luck, and I said, "Au revoir till twelve o'clock." The others snored peacefully.

Gammer Sing and the fifty Hunza Levies were ready, and I had put some chupatties into my haversack overnight, so off we went. By the time we were clear of the village, it was getting light, so, keeping close to the edge of the hills, we struck up a side nullah, took a slant across it, and then began the climb. By this time it was broad daylight. We kept climbing and gradually working round the face of the hill to the right, until we struck the snow line, and I calculated we were pretty well as high as any sangar the enemy might have on the hill. My idea was to get above them, and I didn't want my party swept into space by a stone avalanche. Still, to make matters secure, I detached ten men to go higher up still, and I had five minutes' halt to give them a start.

It was now about 7.30 A.M., and I wanted to push on, so as to be well on the right rear of the enemy by nine o'clock. Once there, we could time our attack at our leisure. Events, however, worked out somewhat differently. The ground now got very bad, and presently we came to a stone shoot which extended high up above us, while ending in a cliff a little below. This we crossed carefully, one man going at a time. Each step set the whole slide in motion and brought stones bounding down from above. The best way was to take it at a rush. We got safely across that, and the ground got worse and worse, and finally we were brought to a halt. I sent men to find a path above and below, the remainder sat down under cover, while I examined the ground in front with my glasses. It was eight o'clock now, and I was congratulating myself in having got so far, as another half-mile would bring us on to a spur which ran down on the right flank of the enemy's line.

As I was looking at this spur, I noticed that there was a nice grassy slope just about level with us, and below that the cliffs went almost sheer down into the river. Once on that slope, we could pretty well play skittles with the sangars below, as we could even now see clearly into them. Unfortunately, the ground between looked frightful, a series of ridges like the teeth of a saw, the northern faces being covered with snow, which made the going particularly treacherous. I had hardly noticed this when there was a puff of smoke and a report, and I saw to my disgust that on the edge of my nice grassy slope were a few clusters of innocent-looking rocks, which I now saw to be sangars, evidently occupied. Just at this moment a man ran across the slope and began waving his coat to someone below, and more men showed themselves among the rocks.

The Levies were still looking for a path, and Humayun wanted to return the enemy's fire; but as the Levies were armed only with carbines, and I hadn't heard the whistle of the enemy's shot, I judged it would be a waste of ammunition. To get the distance, I told Gammer Sing, who had his Martini, to try a shot at the man waving his choga, with his sights at eight hundred yards. I saw the bullet kick the dust to the right of the man, who jumped for a rock, so I knew carbines were no good at that distance.

A path was now found a little lower down, so I ordered an advance and on we went. Our appearance was the signal for the enemy to open fire, but as only one or two bullets sang over us, I knew they couldn't have many rifles. We worked on steadily forward to about five hundred yards, when shots began to drop among us, so under cover of a ridge I divided the men into two groups, and sent the first group forward under cover of the fire of the second, until the first group reached the next ridge, when they covered the advance of the second group.

The ground was shocking bad, and what made it more annoying was that, as we were attacking towards the north, and the snow lay on the northern slopes, we had to test our way every step, and keep in single file just when our advance was most exposed. I had to have a man in places to help me along. I don't mind bad ground when after mahkor, as you can take your own time, but I strongly object to taking the place of the mahkor. Our advance never stopped, but by ten o'clock we had only gone some two hundred yards, and I could see our force crossing the river on to the plain below.

The enemy in our front now began to get excited, and we saw several of them run back and make signals to those below. There was now only one ridge between us and the enemy, and we made for it. As we rose, the enemy's fire became pretty warm, but we were soon under cover again, and as our advanced men gained the ridge, they began firing and yelling as hard as they could go. I thought something was up, so made a rush, a slip, and a scramble, and I could see over the ridge as the rear party came scrambling along. I soon saw the cause of the yelling. About a hundred yards in front of us was the grassy ridge, and across this the last of the enemy was bolting, and in a few minutes had disappeared amid the most appalling yells from the Levies. That was the last our party saw of them, for we now found our path again blocked up by a precipice and again I had to send men above and below to find a practicable way. I then called for a return of casualties, and found we had escaped scot free (I expect the enemy had too). So thus ended our bloodless battle.

While a path was being looked for, Humayun and I sat down in a quiet corner and shared chupatties, and watched the fight below, which was just beginning. First we saw the advance guard get on to the plain and extend, and presently they were joined by the main body, and the whole formed up for attack; then the firing line extended and the advance commenced. Presently we saw the sangars open fire, answered by volleys from our men. Then came a larger puff of smoke and a murmur from the men round me, as a shell pitched across the river and burst over a sangar. It was as pretty a sight as one could wish for, and I felt as if I should have been in a stall at Drury Lane. I could have stopped and watched the show with pleasure. It was quite a treat to see how steadily the 32nd Pioneers worked across the plain; but just then the men below shouted that they had found a path, while I could see those above working their way on to the grassy slope. These latter now shouted that there were no enemy left on the hill, so we chose the lower road, and gradually worked our way down, joining the grassy spur lower down--only it wasn't grassy here at all, but chiefly precipice. We got down somehow, chiefly on all fours, but by the time we had reached the sangars, the enemy had bolted, and they were occupied by our men. It had taken us nearly an hour to get down. Here I came across Colonel Kelly, and after shaking hands, I looked at my watch and found it was just twelve, so I had made a good shot at the time of our meeting when we parted in the morning.

Now I will give you an account of the attack carried out by the main body. It is the official account, so I can back its correctness.

The action at Chokalwat on the 9th April is thus described: "On the morning of the ninth April I advanced to the attack of the enemy. In the early morning Lieutenant Beynon, with the Hunza Levies, ascended the high hills on the left bank of the river to turn the right of the position and attack in rear. The Punyal Levies were sent up the hills on the right bank to turn out the men above the stone shoots.

"I advanced in the following manner:--

```
Half Coy. 32nd Pioneers, advanced guard.
Kashmir Sappers and Miners          --
Half Company 32nd Pioneers          |
Two guns 1st Kashmir Mountain       |= Main Body
Battery, carried by coolies         |
One Company 32nd Pioneers           --
```

"The baggage, under escort of the rearguard, remained in Gasht till ordered forward after the action.

"An advance was made to the river, where the bridge had been broken, but sufficiently repaired by the Sappers and Miners for the passage of the infantry. The guns forded the river, and the force ascended to the fan facing the right sangars of the enemy's position.

"The configuration of the ground was as follows: The road from the river after leaving Gasht brought us on to an alluvial fan, the ascent to which was short and steep; it was covered with boulders and intersected with nullahs; the road led across this fan and then along the foot of steep shale slopes and shoots, within five hundred yards of the line of sangars crowning the opposite side of the river bank, and totally devoid of any sort or description of cover for some two miles; it could also be swept by avalanches of stones set in motion by a few men placed on the heights above for that purpose.

"The enemy's position consisted of a line of sangars blocking the roads from the river up to the alluvial fan on which they were placed. The right of the position was protected by a snow glacier, which descended into the river bed, and furthermore by sangars, which extended into the snow line up the spur of the hills.

"The course of the action was as follows: The advanced guard formed up at about eight hundred yards from the position and the main body in rear. The 32nd Pioneers then advanced to the attack. One section, 'C' Company, extended (left of line). One section, 'C' Company, extended in support. Two sections, 'C' Company, 'A' Company, in reserve. The guns now took up position on the right and opened on 'A' sangar at a range of eight hundred and twenty-five yards. As the action progressed, the supporting section of 'C' Company advanced and reinforced. The remaining half of 'C' Company advanced, and, leaving sufficient space for the guns, took up their position in the firing line on the extreme right. Volley firing at first was opened at eight hundred yards, but the firing line advanced one hundred and fifty to two hundred yards as the action progressed. At a later stage, one section of 'A' Company was pushed up to fill a gap on the right of the guns in action in the centre of the line. The enemy, after receiving some well-directed volleys and correctly played shells, were seen to vacate 'A' sangar by twos and threes until it was finally emptied. During our advance to the fan, shots were heard in the direction of the hills, Lieutenant Beynon having come into contact with the enemy in their sangars up the hillside, who were driven from ridge to ridge. When 'A' sangar was vacated, attention was directed on 'B' sangar, and the same course adopted, with the same result; at the same time those driven down from the hills above streamed into the plain, and there was then a general flight. Six shrapnel were fired into the flying enemy at ranges of a thousand, twelve hundred, and thirteen hundred and fifty yards (three rounds per gun).

"A general advance was then made down precipitous banks to the bed of the river, covered by the fire of the reserves, the river forded, and sangars 'A' and 'B' occupied. The guns were then carried across, and, the whole line of sangars having been vacated, the column was re-formed on the fan; the line taken in crossing enabled the enemy to get well on their way to Mastuj; the advance was then continued to a village a mile and a half farther along the river, where a halt was made. The casualties consisted of one man of the 32nd Pioneers severely wounded, and three Kashmir Sappers slightly. The action commenced at 10.30 A.M. and lasted one hour. The position was of unusual natural strength, and the disposition of the sangars showed considerable tactical ability, being placed on the edge of high cliffs on the left bank of the river. The enemy were computed at four to five hundred, and were armed with Martini-Henry and Snider rifles. Several dead were found in the sangars, and the losses I estimate to have been from fifty to sixty."

By the time I had joined Colonel Kelly, the Pioneers had re-formed and were advancing, so I had very little time to take a look at the sangars. I saw one or two bodies lying around, and the shells seemed to have knocked sparks pretty successfully out of the stone breastworks. I also noticed the neat little cooking places the enemy had made behind their sangars, showing that they had been there for some time.

The advance was carried on without a check for about one and a half miles, when we came to a cluster of huts near the termination of the plain, the river here making a slight sweep towards the left side of the valley. An advance guard was thrown out well to the front, and under their protection the column halted and the men fell out. I had a first-class thirst by this time, and Gammer Sing made several trips to the river before it was quenched. Gammer Sing and I always share the same tin mug on the march. It is his mug, but he always gives me first go. In return I supply Gammer Sing with tobacco, so it is a fair division of labour. Here I finished my chupatties, and some kind man--I think it was Borradaile--gave me a stick of chocolate, my own store having run out, but I managed to get it replenished at Mastuj.

Good old Stewart came up as pleased as Punch at having had his first fight. Said he, "And d'ye think now that me shells killed many of the beggars? sure and their corpses ought to be just thick." He was pained to hear that in all probability we should not catch up the enemy again that day, I really think nothing less than twelve hours' hard fighting every day, with short intervals for refreshments, would satisfy him.

One of the guns, when being brought up the cliff, had slipped off the coolies and fallen down to the bottom again, breaking off the foresight, but Stewart mended it during the halt.

At the same time, the Sappers were hard at work pulling down a house for materials to build a bridge, but before it was actually begun, we heard that the river could be forded again lower down, so the bridge was not built. By this time the men were sufficiently rested, the whole column had closed up, and orders sent back for the baggage to come on.

Off we started, the Punyal Levies working down the right bank, the Hunzas on the left, the main column following the left bank of the stream. By 4 P.M. we reached the ford and crossed to the right bank, the water not being much above our knees. And almost immediately after, we saw some men drawn up on the spur we were approaching; they turned out to be the Mastuj garrison, who, on finding the besieging force halting, had come out to find out the reason. If they had only heard our guns and turned out at once, they would have cut the line of retreat of our opponents, and the whole crew must have been wiped out. Unfortunately the fort of Mastuj is built far down the reverse slope of a fan, and although some of the sentries reported they heard firing, it was thought they must be mistaken.

By 5 P.M. we had got on to the spur, and found Moberly, with part of the garrison, all looking very fat and fit; evidently the siege had not worried them much so far. A detachment of the 14th Sikhs (the remains of Ross's company) were left on the spur to cover the baggage coming in, while our column trotted down to the fort, getting there by 5.30 P.M. Here we found Jones with his arm in a sling. Our force bivouacked in a garden attached to the fort, the trees of which had been lopped to deprive the enemy of shelter, and the farther wall destroyed. This we precious soon built up again, and within an hour our force was comfortably entrenched and cooking its dinner.

What a blessing it was to be down again in a decent climate! Fires were still pleasant at night, but in the daytime the bright, cool weather was splendid.

Moberly's servant soon had some tea and chupatties ready, and while we were eating them, Bretherton, who had been out clearing some village on the other side of the fort, came in.

There was lots of news, both to hear and relate, and we were hard at it when there came the sound of a volley from the direction in which we were expecting the baggage.

Somebody said, "Cuss those niggers! why can't they let us have our tea in peace?"--it wasn't Stewart,--and there was a general scramble for swords and belts. A company of the Pioneers was soon doubling off, while the rest of us strolled up the road to see what the row was. We met the baggage coming in, and heard that the 14th Sikh picket had heard some people moving in the river bed, and had let drive a volley at them--result unknown. As soon as the last of the baggage had passed, we followed it, and the picket was withdrawn. Later that night we sent back a messenger with an account of the day's fighting and the relief of Mastuj to Gilgit, but the messenger--a levy--shortly returned, having been fired on, and returned the fire, so it was evident that a good many of the enemy were still sneaking about.

We officers slept in the fort that night, four or five of us in a room. Mastuj is of the ordinary type of country fort, square, with a tower at each end and one over the gateway, curtains between each tower about eighteen to twenty feet high, and the towers another fifteen feet higher still. The whole place is built of layers of stones and wood plastered together with mud, while there is generally a keep or citadel inside which commands the rest of the fort, and in which are the governor's and women's quarters. In Mastuj, of course, we used these as officers' quarters. The whole fort is a horribly dirty and tumble-down old place; the roof of the officers' quarters had to be propped up, as it was considered unsafe, and I quite believe it. The rooms had the usual hole in the roof for the smoke to get out at, but Moberly had erected a stove in his room, which was a great improvement.

CHAPTER VI
THE RECONNAISSANCE FROM MASTUJ

While at Mastuj we heard from Jones the story of the disaster at Koragh--which I will give.

Ross, with Jones and about ninety-three Sikhs, left Mastuj on the 7th March, with the intention of helping Edwardes and Fowler, who were believed to be in danger at Reshun, and marched to Buni; leaving a detachment there of thirty-three sepoys under a native officer, he marched with Jones and sixty men for Reshun, hoping to arrive there that day.

After leaving Buni, the road runs for some distance along flat ground until the junction of the Turikho and Yarkhun rivers is reached. At this point the road leads up along the face of a cliff and then down on to a small plain, where are a few houses and some patches of cultivation. This is known as the village of Koragh, and immediately after, the river runs between the cliffs, which draw together and make the mouth of the defile. The path which follows the left bank crosses the debris fallen from the cliffs above and then runs along the edge of the river at the foot of another and smaller cliff, or in summer, when the river is full, the path runs over this smaller cliff. Ross's party took the lower road. After the second cliff the paths lead on to a small plain about two hundred yards wide at its greatest width, and perhaps half a mile long, and then runs up and across the face of a third cliff which drops sheer down into the river. This cliff forms the end of the trap. It would be hard to find a better place for an ambuscade.

Ross's advance guard was on this plain, approaching the spur which closes the trap, when they were fired on. Ross went forward to reconnoitre the ground, and at once saw the impossibility of driving the enemy out with his small force, and therefore ordered Jones to go back and hold the entrance of the defile to enable them to escape. On the first shot being fired, the coolies had chucked their loads and bolted, as likely as not helping to man the sangars enclosing the party. Jones, taking ten men, made an attempt to reach the mouth of the defile, but found it already occupied by the enemy, who had run up stone sangars, and by the time he had got within a hundred yards of it, eight of his ten men were wounded. He therefore fell back on the main party, who had taken refuge in some caves at the foot of the cliff.

The caves, now half full of water, owing to the rising of the river, can be seen in the photograph. The party remained in these caves till 9 P.M., when they made another attempt to cut their way out, but were driven back by avalanches of stones. They then had to scale the mountainside, but were stopped by an impossible cliff, and one sepoy, falling over, was killed, so they came back to the caves dead tired. Here they remained the whole of the next day, the enemy trying an occasional shot from across the river, where they had erected sangars; but the Sikhs had, in their turn, built sangars across the mouth of their cave, which sheltered them.

Then the enemy tried rolling stones over the top of the cliff, but this only had the effect of strengthening the sangars, so they shut that up.

During that day, Ross and Jones came to the conclusion that there was nothing to be done but cut their way out; everyone must take his chance, the rush to be made about 2 A.M. On the morning of the 10th, accordingly, at the time fixed, they made their sortie.

A heavy fire was at once opened on them from both sides of the river, while avalanches of stones were sent hurtling down the cliffs. A number of sepoys were killed or knocked senseless by stones, but the remainder reached the sangars, and cleared out the defenders at the point of the bayonet. Here poor Ross was killed by a bullet through the head, after having, so the natives say, pistolled some four of the enemy. The latter, after being driven out of the sangars, bolted up the hillside, and again opened fire from among the rocks. By the time the small band reached the maidan, there were only some seventeen men, headed by Jones: of these, Jones and nine others were wounded.

Here the little party formed up, and tried to help any more of their friends who might be struggling through, by heavy volley-firing into the sangars on both sides of the river. After some ten minutes of thus waiting, during which they twice drove off attacks of the enemy's swordsmen, who tried to close with them, and losing three more men, Jones, noticing an attempt of the enemy to cut the line of retreat, and despairing of any more of the detachment escaping, gave the order to retire. This was carried out slowly and leisurely till they reached Buni, at about 6 A.M., when they joined the detachment they had left behind. Jones and his party remained in Buni till the 17th, the enemy not daring to attack them, and they were unable to move, having no transport for their wounded.

After Ross had left Mastuj, Moberly remained in command of the fort, and on the 10th March was joined by Captain Bretherton of the Commissariat who came in with two sepoys from Ghizr.

Moberly heard that Ross had left a small party at Buni, and though he sent messengers to this party, he never received any reply, the messengers probably being captured.

On the 13th, hearing that the enemy were occupying the Nisa Gol, a position some six miles from Mastuj, he reconnoitred up to it, and found some sangars, which he destroyed, but no enemy.

A reinforcement of sixty sepoys came in that day from Ghizr. The next two days were spent in trying to collect coolies for transport, and on the 16th, in spite of the non-arrival of any coolies, he set out to Buni with a hundred and fifty sepoys, each man carrying a sheepskin coat, two blankets, a hundred and twenty rounds of ammunition, and three days' cooked rations.

He halted that night at Sanoghar, where he collected some fifty coolies, and learned by signal from Mastuj that Bretherton was sending some fifty Yarkhun coolies the next day--fifty Punyal Levies also joined him that evening. Starting the next morning, he reached Buni by 5 P.M., when he found Jones and the remains of the Sikhs. The return journey was begun two hours later, at 7 P.M., and carried on steadily all night, a small body of the enemy following, but not daring to attack. Mastuj was reached between 10 and 11 A.M. the next day, 18th March.

By the 22nd March the enemy had surrounded the fort, and the siege began. Nothing of any event happened, the enemy contenting themselves with long-range firing, only one man being slightly wounded and two ponies killed. On the 9th of April "up we came with our little lot," and the siege was raised.

Early the next morning we were up and going through the state of the supplies and available amount of transport.

Transport and supplies were an everlasting source of worry, as it generally is with every army, great or small.

We soon got a return of the supplies in Mastuj. I forget how many days it was, but none too much for our force and the Mastuj garrison. Bretherton was sent back to bring up supplies from the rear, and messengers were sent to order in the villagers. We wanted their grain to eat, and men to carry it. The villagers began to come in after a bit, and brought a small amount of grain with them.

Stewart was hard at work getting ponies for his guns in place of the mules left behind; the gun wheel and carriage saddles were sent for, and shortly arrived.

The Levies were billeted in the houses which had lately been occupied by the enemy, and we soon had pickets out round the fort. In showing the Levies the houses they were to occupy, I examined the enemy's system of loopholes and sangars, and found they were very well made indeed. In the house which had lately been occupied by Mahomed Issar, their commander-in-chief we found the trunk of a tree which the enemy were converting into a cannon. It didn't require cannon to bring the walls of Mastuj down,--a good strong kick would have been quite sufficient. Shortly after we had reached Chitral, Moberly reported that part of the wall had fallen on a sleeping sepoy, who was luckily saved by some beams catching and protecting him from being crushed by the debris. There was no apparent cause for the collapse, but the man is supposed to have sneezed.

The next day a fatigue party was sent out to Chokalwat to destroy the enemy's sangars, and bury any dead bodies that might be lying about. This party would also act as a covering party to Peterson, who was expected to arrive that day. With Peterson came Bethune and Luard, all very sick at having missed a fight. This detachment brought the strength of the Pioneers up to four hundred rifles.

The Hunza and fifty Punyal Levies were sent to reconnoitre towards Nisa Gol that day, and fifty more Punyals up the Yarkhun valley to forage. The rest of the day was spent in writing reports, making out official returns, and other necessary nuisances.

Colonel Kelly and I were writing in a tent pitched on the roof, and I had pretty well got through my work by 5 P.M.; and then Colonel Kelly had out the maps and returns of supplies, etc., and, Borradaile being called, there was a small council of war.

As I have before said, Colonel Kelly had practically settled at Pingal to advance by Killa Drasan, but the question was, when should we be in a position to do so? Here came in that everlasting transport and supply question. We could now, of course, cut down our baggage by leaving behind warm clothes and poshteens, as the weather would be getting hotter every day as we descended to lower latitudes; but this only meant that the men would have to carry less themselves, and, try as we would, it seemed as if we could only raise enough transport for seven days' supplies, five on coolies and two days in the men's haversacks. It was seven days' march to Chitral by the direct route, and though our intelligence pointed to the fact that supplies in the Chitral fort were probably plentiful, it was yet only summer. Then, again, we might, or we might not, get supplies on the road. We worried the question up and down and inside out, but we couldn't increase the transport by one coolie. Borradaile was for going on. I said, "The first man in Chitral gets a C.B."

Just then Raja Akbar Khan and Humayun came back, so we went out to hear their report. Old Akbar smiled a fat smile all over his face, and Humayun twirled his long moustache,--he has a fine black beard and moustache and a deep bass voice. Akbar Khan curls his beard like an Assyrian king, and smiles good-naturedly at everything.

They reported that they had seen the enemy building sangars, and that there were many men, also cavalry. Their report was clear enough, and from their description I could pretty well place the position of the different sangars, as I had been over the ground with Harley on my previous visit to Chitral. To make matters certain, I suggested that I should reconnoitre the position next day. This was agreed to, and it was also determined to attack the enemy on the 13th April, as it was no use giving them time to entrench themselves more than we could help.

I started off about 9 A.M. on the morning of the 12th April, mounted on a transport pony. I had about fifty Hunza and Punyal Levies, under Humayun and Akbar Khan, with me; these two also had ponies, Akbar Khan having managed to get two over the pass with great difficulty. It was a lovely morning, and we were all very cheerful except Gammer Sing, who wanted to come along with me; but as he had to get my kit sorted and put right for the next day's march, I left him behind, but took his rifle and ammunition.

We dropped over the bluff and forded the Laspur stream, which was hardly over the men's knees, and then kept along the bed of the river, with a few scouts well up the hills on our left, the Mastuj or Yarkhun river protecting our right. After about two miles we came to a small homestead and Humayun told me there was a wounded man inside; so in I went, and found the poor beggar with his right leg smashed by a bullet just above the knee. There were a lot of women and children and two men in the house, his brothers, so I gave them a note to Luard, and told them to carry the man into Mastuj, which they did. Luard set his leg, and by this time he is no doubt well and happy.

Shortly after that, we climbed up from the bed of the river on to a narrow ledge which ran along the foot of the hills about two hundred feet above the river. Here we left our horses, and went scrambling along among the fallen debris for about half a mile, when we came to the foot of a stone slope, and I noticed our advanced guard had halted on the top, and on asking the reason, Humayun said that the enemy were occupying the next spurs. So up we went, and found the fact true enough, but the next spur was some thousand yards away; so on we went across that slope, and on to the next, eventually reaching a very nice little place some eight hundred yards from the spur occupied by the enemy.

From here I could see pretty well the whole of the position occupied by the enemy, except the end of the Nisa Gol nullah where it debouches on to the river. I tried going up the hill, but that only made matters worse, so I determined to sketch what I could see from here, and then try across the river. In order not to be interrupted, I sent five men well up the hill on to a spur, from whence they could see any man who tried to sneak up for a shot, and spread out the rest in skirmishing order to my front. Humayun and Akbar got behind a rock and went to sleep, and I got out my telescope and set to work.

The enemy seemed rather interested in our proceedings--we could see their heads bobbing up and down behind the sangars; but after we had settled down, they gradually took courage, and, coming outside, sat down to watch us. This was very nice of them, for very soon I had a complete list of the garrison of each sangar, and from where I was could see the sort of gun they were armed with,--a few rifles among the lower sangars, and nearly all matchlocks among the higher and more inaccessible ones. It was a calm, peaceful scene: the enemy sitting outside their sangars sunning themselves; and my men lying down, a few watching, the rest sleeping, one or two enjoying a friendly pipe.

Shortly after, we saw two gallant young sparks come riding along the plain on the opposite side of the river, evidently having been sent by the general to report on our proceedings. They pulled up opposite us and watched us for a short time, and then one slipped off his horse, which was led by the other behind a big boulder. Thinking they would merely watch us, I shouted to my men to keep an eye on them, and went on sketching. Presently there was a bang, and ping came a bullet over our heads. The beggar was potting at us at about a thousand yards, unpardonable waste of ammunition! I put a rock between us, and went on sketching, everyone else did ditto, and presently our friend shut up, but after a time, finding things slow, I suppose, he began again. This seemed to annoy Humayun, who asked for the loan of my rifle, and he and Akbar went dodging down the hill. They disappeared behind a dip in the ground, and presently I saw them come out lower down among some bushes, and gradually they worked their way down to the edge of the river about eight hundred yards from our friend, who was calmly sitting in the open, having occasional pot shots at us, while his friend had come out and was evidently criticising the performance.

Presently there was a bang from our side of the river, and a spurt of dust on the opposite maidan where the bullet struck. Humayun had over-judged the distance. By the time he was ready for another shot, our two friends were legging it across the plain as fast as their ponies could gallop. He got in a couple of shots more, but they did not hurt anybody.

As soon as Humayun commenced firing, the sangars in our front began humming like a beehive and presently shot after shot came dropping among us; the enemy evidently had plenty of ammunition, and for some minutes things were quite lively; but, finding we made no response, they calmed down gradually, and peace once more reigned supreme.

I chaffed old Humayun, when he came back, on his shooting powers, and he grinned in response.

I now noticed rather a commotion among the garrison of the sangars across the Nisa Gol nullah; the men began turning out, and one or two ran towards the higher sangars, evidently passing on some news. Presently I saw a crowd of men, mostly mounted, with others on foot carrying flags. Then came a fat man in white, with a standard-bearer all to himself. All the garrisons of the sangars turned out, and I counted them--there were over a hundred in each.

The commander-in-chief rode up the whole length of the nullah, and then walked up the spur on which are shown sangars Nos. 16 and 17 in the sketch. Here he sat down, and, I have no doubt, calculated the odds on his winning when the action came off. After a time he came down the hill, and the procession moved down along the nullah and out of sight.

When I had finished my sketch, I shut up my telescope and said--

"Now we'll go across the river."

"Why do you want to cross the river?" said Humayun.

"I want to see the end of the nullah," said I.

"Their cavalry will get you," said he.

"What cavalry?" said I.

"You've just seen two of them," said he.

"Get out!" said I; "you're pulling my leg."

"Don't go," said he.

"I'm going," said I.

"Where the Sahib goes, I follow," said he.

"Come on, Ruth," said I. "'Whither thou goest, I will go!' I've heard that remark before."

These hillmen have an extraordinarily exaggerated idea of cavalry. Any young buck on a long-tailed screw is a Chevalier Bayard to them. Why, you've only to move ten yards to your right or left in any part of the country, and no cavalry could reach you, while you could sit and chuck stones at them.

Down we dropped again into the river bed, leaving a few men to signal any movement of the enemy while we were crossing. We had our ponies brought up and rode across the stream, the men fording, then we scrambled up the high slope of the opposite bank and shouted for the remainder to follow.

A short distance up the hill, and I could see the end of the nullah, with a large sangar covering the road. This was what I wished to know, so, after a careful look, having seen all I wanted, we started homewards by the opposite bank to that by which we had come, crossing the river again by a bridge which Oldham had been employed the day before in mending, and reached Mastuj by 1 P.M.

I gave in my report to Colonel Kelly, and then got out orders for the next day's march.

I also suggested that some light scaling ladders should be made, as I expected we should find them very useful in crossing the Nisa Gol. Accordingly, Oldham set his Sappers to work, and by evening had ten light scaling ladders ready, each about ten feet long, and light enough to be carried by one man.

A certain amount of supplies and some coolies had been collected. The guns had been mounted on ponies, and could now march along faster than when carried by coolies.

Everything was ready for an early advance the next morning, so as a little diversion we were photographed by Moberly. Moberly was coming out the next day in command of a company of Kashmir troops; after the expected fight, he would return to Mastuj to resume command, and the Kashmir troops would be put under my charge.

The orders for next day were to march at 7 A.M., baggage to remain in Mastuj till sent for, and then to come out under escort of part of the garrison, who would escort back any wounded we might have, Luard coming out in charge of the field hospital and returning with the wounded to form a base hospital at Mastuj.

I managed to get a bottle of whiskey out of Moberly. It belonged, I believe, to Fowler, but as he was either a prisoner or dead, he wouldn't require the whiskey. I also replenished my store of chocolate.

CHAPTER VII
THE FIGHT AT NISA GOL

Next morning, 13th April, we were all having a good square breakfast by 6 A.M., and punctually at seven o'clock the column moved off, headed by the Levies.

Our force consisted of--

400 Pioneers, 100 Kashmir Infantry,
40 Kashmir Sappers,
2 Mountain guns,
100 Hunza and Punyal Levies;

rather less than a single battalion, and not much with which to force our way through seventy miles of bad country, but still we were determined to get to Chitral before the Peshawur force.

It was a perfect morning, nice bright sunshine, and a jolly fresh feeling in the air, sort of day that makes you want to take a gun and go shooting; in fact, just the very day for a fight.

The Levies were across Oldham's bridge in no time, but the Pioneers had to cross it slowly, as it was very jumpy, and only four men could be allowed on it at a time. The guns were sent up to a ford some three hundred yards up the stream. After crossing the main stream there was still a creek to be forded, but this was not much above the men's knees. This gave the Levies time to get ahead and send some scouts up the hills to the right, in order to give timely warning if the enemy should try on the rolling stone dodge, but the hills just here did not lend themselves very readily to this mode of warfare. When our little army got across the river, the advance guard was halted and the column formed up, and then on we went. Peterson was in command of the advance guard, with orders to halt when he reached the edge of the plain to allow the column to close up for the attack. On the order to advance he was to hug the hill on his right.

Just before the maidan the road drops down on to the river bed, and then runs up on to the maidan itself, which gradually slopes up to the centre, where it is divided by a deep nullah that I think they call in America a canon. The sides of this nullah are in most places perpendicular, varying from two hundred and fifty to three hundred feet in depth, with a small stream running along the bottom, the amount of water depending on the melting of the snow in the hills above. There are two places to cross it, one the regular road to Chitral, which zig-zags down the nullah near the mouth, and the other a goat track about half-way between the road and the hills. Both of these had sangars covering their approach on the enemy's side of the nullah, and any attempt to rush them would have led to great loss of life.

To the casual observer the plain looks perfectly flat, but as a matter of fact the slope is rather more pronounced at the foot than at the top near the hills, with the result that from the sangar covering the main road, the upper end of the plain is partially hidden from fire.

The plain also is really a succession of what may be described as waves running parallel with the nullah, which afford very excellent shelter to any attacking force. In fact, the only obstacle is the nullah; but, as you may see from the photos, this obstacle is no small one, and could only be crossed by two paths as far as we knew. Our object was to find another path, and to get to close quarters with the enemy.

So much for the ground: now for the fight. Peterson and the Levies got on to the maidan and extended, while the main body formed up for attack. Then the order to advance was given, and off we went.

Peterson and the Levies were in the firing line and extended, the Levies on the right.

As the remaining companies reached the level plain, they first formed into line and went forward in the regular everyday style. The ground was very nice for parade movements, a gentle, grassy slope with plenty of room. The Levies, however, were not keeping close enough to the hillside, and were gradually pushing Peterson's company off to the left, where they would have been exposed to the fire of the big sangar plus the flanking fire from the sangars up the spur on the left bank of the river.

Colonel Kelly accordingly sent me off to change their direction more to the right, and to close the Levies until they were wanted. I found Humayun's pony taking shelter under a rock, so, mounting it, I galloped after Peterson, gave him the order, and then closed the Levies on their right. This made a gap into which we of the supporting companies pushed, so now we had two companies in the firing line, two in support, and the Kashmir Company in reserve. In this formation we pushed on till we came under fire of the sangars, and had reached the valley running up into the hills, about four hundred yards from the nullah, thus again giving room for the Levies to form line on the right of the Pioneers.

The fun now began as the enemy started plugging away at us from the sangars on the spur, but not much at present from the lower ones, as only the flank of Peterson's company could be seen.

Stewart had got his guns into action and was shelling sangar No. 16. After a time Peterson engaged the sangars on the maidan, and they gave him a pretty warm time of it.

The Levies opened fire at three hundred yards, rather close range to begin an action, and it was very amusing watching them; their instruction in volley-firing had only just been begun, but they had entire faith in its efficiency.

The section commanders used to give the word to load in their own language, but the order to fire was "fira vollee," and they were supposed to fire on the word "vollee." If any man fired before the order,--and they frequently did,--the section commander used to rush at the culprit and slap him severely on the nearest part of him. As the Levies were lying down, the slaps were--on the usual place.

After a time the fire from the sangar slackened, and as things seemed to be going all right, I stopped the Levies firing, and, taking two of them, went forward up to the edge of the nullah to see if there was any sign of a road. We followed the edge upwards for some two hundred yards, and then I told the two levies to go on until they found a place, and then went back.

The fire from the sangar had recommenced, as Stewart's attention had been turned towards others, so Colonel Kelly sent orders to Stewart to send in one or two more shells, which had the desired effect.

I now sent Gammer Sing to get a fresh supply of ammunition for the Levies, which he brought, and I then followed Colonel Kelly down the line to the Pioneers.

In the meantime the guns had changed their position, and were engaged with the lower sangars, as was also Peterson, who, I think, was under the hottest fire the whole time, as he had the attention of two big sangars entirely paid to him. The guns also got hit a bit, and among others two of the drivers were killed; they were the owners of the gun ponies, and remained with the ponies under a guard of four Kashmir sepoys, who had commands to shoot any man trying to bolt. They and their ponies of course made a large target, but the ponies also acted as a protection. One more of the Pioneer companies now came into the firing line, and these three companies devoted their entire attention to one sangar, whose fire was now very intermittent.

I now got Colonel Kelly's leave to go and look for a path, and hailed Oldham to come and help me work forward therefore in front of the firing line, to do which we had to ask Borradaile to stop one company firing, which he very kindly did. We struck the nullah close opposite the empty sangar No. 15, and from there followed the edge till we were well within sight of the sangars in the middle of the maidan, without having found a place where we could get down, but we noticed a track which led up the opposite bank. We therefore turned back and retraced our steps till we came to a spot which we had examined before, but had thought impossible. Where we stood the drop was sheer for some seventy feet, but then there came a ledge, from which we thought we could scramble down on to the bed of the stream and up the opposite side, where we had noticed the track. We therefore hurried back; Oldham for his Sappers, and I to report to Colonel Kelly. I likewise asked for the reserve company of Kashmir troops to cross over as soon as a path could be made under cover of the fire of the already extended companies of the Pioneers. Colonel Kelly assented, and I sent off a note to Moberly to bring up his company. When I got back to the nullah, I found the Pioneers extended along the edge, and Oldham's Sappers already at work.

The Levies in the meantime had heard of a path higher up in the hills, and were sent off to cross as best they could. Having nothing more to do, I sat down where Oldham's men were at work, and watched the proceedings. The men in No. 16 sangar had evidently had enough of it, their sangar having been pretty well knocked about their ears, and when any of the survivors tried a shot, it called down a volley on him. Presently they began to bolt, and then the laugh was on our side.

That sangar was a death-trap to its garrison--their only line of escape was across some open, shaley slopes within four hundred yards of our firing line, and the Levies were now working along the hill, and would catch them in the sangar if they didn't clear out. The result was like rabbit shooting You'd see a man jump from the sangar and bolt across the shale slope, slipping and scrambling as he went; then there would be a volley, and you'd see the dust fly all round him--perhaps he'd drop, perhaps he wouldn't; then there would be another volley, and you'd see him chuck forward amid a laugh from the sepoys, and he'd roll over and over till he'd fetch up against a rock and lie still. Sometimes two or three would bolt at once; one or two would drop at each volley, and go rolling, limp and shapeless down the slope, until they were all down, and there would be a wait for the next lot. An old sepoy lying near me declared as each man dropped that it was his particular rifle whose aim had been so accurate, until Borradaile called him sharply to order, and told him to attend to business. Presently a crowd of men appeared higher up on the same spur, and someone called out that they were Levies. Just then one of them dropped on his knee and fired in our direction, there was a volley back, and the men disappeared again.

Oldham had now managed, with ropes and the scaling ladders, to get down on to the ledge below, so calling to Moberly to bring along his company, I dived down, followed by Gammer Sing and then Moberly, and one or two men of the Sappers followed him, and we, thinking the whole company was coming, went scrambling down to the bottom. We slid down the ropes on to the ladders, and from them on to the ledge, followed it a bit along the cliff, and then down a shale and debris slope to the stream, across that and up the other side. Scrambling on all fours up the opposite side, I heard Oldham, who was ahead of me, shout back that the company wasn't following. I yelled, "Run up a sangar, and we can hold on till they come," and finished my scramble up to the top.

Then we took a look round to see how things stood.

Devil a sign of the company coming down the rope was there, and the Pioneers seemed to have disappeared too.

Then we numbered our party--three British officers, my orderly, and eleven Sappers, the latter armed with Snider carbines only; my orderly was the only one with a bayonet. There was a low ridge in front of us hiding the enemy's sangars, so we lined this with the Sappers, till we could see what the game was. We now saw the Pioneers moving down the nullah towards the river, while at the same time the Levies showed on the ridge and took possession of the sangar. We were all right, I saw, so I gave the order to advance--keeping along the edge of the nullah so as to get at the sangars. Of course just my luck that as we started to advance, the buckle of my chuplie broke; there was no time to mend it, so I shoved it into my haversack, and went along with one bare foot; luckily the ground was not very stony.

As soon as we topped the swell of the ground, we saw the enemy bolting in twos and threes from the nearest sangar, now about two hundred yards off, and presently there came a rush right across our front. We opened fire, trying volleys at first, but the Sappers were useless at that, never having had any training, so independent firing was ordered. During the halt Moberly had a narrow shave, a bullet passing between his left hand and thigh, as he was standing superintending the firing. His hand was almost touching his thigh, and the bullet raised the skin of the palm just below the little finger.

The nearest sangar was now pretty well empty, and the Pioneers from the other side of the nullah were firing obliquely across our front, rather too close to be pleasant; so we altered our advance half right, so as to cut into the line of retreat of the enemy, and made for a jumble of stones out in the open; by the time we reached it, there was a stream of men flying right across our front, horse and foot, at about five hundred yards, so again we opened fire. Moberly and I both took carbines from the men, as they were firing wildly; the sepoy whose carbine I took invariably managed to jam the cartridge, partly his fault, and partly the fault of the worn state of the extractor. Gammer Sing was plugging in bullets quietly on my right, and gave me the distance as five hundred yards. I knew he was pretty correct, as I watched his bullets pitch. I sang out the distance, and we got merrily to work. Oh, if I had only had a company of my regiment, I think even Stewart would have been satisfied. Precious soon the rush had passed us, and we had to begin putting up our sights, and of course then the cream of the business was over.

About this time Shah Mirza came along, and, seeing me with only one chuplie, offered me his, which I accepted, as it was a matter of indifference to him whether he went barefooted or not. I sent him off to bring up the Levies, who were looting the arms and securing the prisoners from the sangars.

Cobbe now appeared with some few Pioneers, and shortly after, a whole company, but the enemy were now quite out of sight; however, a company was sent in pursuit. Colonel Kelly came up, and we congratulated him, and there was a general demand for cigarettes, Moberly, I believe, being the happy possessor of some. As we were grouped round Colonel Kelly, "whit" came a bullet over us, some idiot up the hill leaving his P.P.C. card, I presume.

One of the first questions I asked was, what had become of the Kashmir Company, and then first heard the following curious incident.

It appears that after the first few of us had gone down the cliff, and the rest were preparing to follow, a bullet struck some cakes of gun-cotton lying on the ground by the head of the path, where they had been placed while the Sappers were at work. The bullet, striking these cakes, ignited them, and they blazed up, and Borradaile, fearing an explosion, ordered a retirement of those troops nearest it to cover some thirty yards in rear, where they were protected by a wave of the ground. The enemy, seeing our men bolting, as they thought, rushed out of their sangars, but were promptly fired into by the Pioneers. Just then the Levies on the ridge and our small party showed across the nullah, threatening their line of retreat; this was apparently more than they had bargained for, so they began to bolt, as I have said. Then the Pioneers moved down the nullah and crossed by the goat track.

Peterson's company had found a box full of Snider ammunition in one of the sangars, so the Kashmir Company was sent back to look for any more, and also to demolish the sangars. I took the opportunity to have a look at them too. I was surprised at the magnificent way in which they were built, partly sunk into the ground, and made of huge boulders that required many men to move, and with head cover constructed of logs in the most approved fashion, evidently made by men who had been properly instructed. As I neared the largest sangar, I saw a native clothed in a red dressing-gown, sitting on the ground with a long native jezail. Rather surprised at seeing one of the enemy thus armed, I went up to him, and as I did so, he picked up his gun. I had my revolver on him in a second, and told him to drop the gun, which he did. I then asked him who he was, and found he was our long-lost child--I mean levy--who had been captured at Laspur. The enemy had not treated him badly, but had taken his carbine and his choga, hence the dressing-gown; in return he had sneaked a gun when the enemy were flying. I set the Kashmir troops to work, and then went back, meeting Humayun and his captives on the way.

"Humayun," I said, "your levy is over there."

"Is he alive?" said Humayun, looking in a most bloodthirsty way at his prisoners.

I assured him he was. Thereupon Humayun gave a jump, caught hold of both my hands, and kissed them violently. I was afraid he was going to kiss my ruby lips, but he didn't. He and Akbar Khan then went scuttling across country to the sangar, followed by a crowd of his men, whooping and yelling with joy.

The guns were now coming across the nullah, and the column was being formed up with the intention of crossing the river to Sanoghar, where it was proposed to camp for the night. Part of the Levies and a company of the Pioneers were sent ahead to clear the village of any evilly disposed persons; arrangements were made for bringing up the sick and wounded; and a signal message was flashed back to Mastuj for the baggage to come out.

The fight was over by 12.30 P.M., so we had only been about two hours from start to finish. Our losses were six killed and sixteen wounded, two of whom died next day. Three of the battery ponies were also killed.

The path down to the river was so steep and the rickety bridge over it so unsafe that it was determined to camp on the side of the river on which we were, especially as we should have to recross the next day.

A camping ground was soon found, pickets thrown out, and the wounded brought in.

A deputation from Sanoghar village was now seen coming across from the opposite bank. Most of the deputation on arrival seemed half naked; we thought this was a sign of humility on their part, but I heard afterwards that the Levies had come across them, and taken their chogas in exchange for that of their man in the red dressing-gown.

This deputation gave the usual yarn about being compelled to fight against us, and how glad they were that we had won.

We made our usual reply, that they could and must show their gladness by providing coolies and supplies, all of which would be paid for. We also made them send over charpoys (beds) for the wounded.

We had taken some twelve prisoners, who came in useful as transport; in fact, until we got to Chitral every man we caught was turned into a beast of burden and given a load; and if he was an Adamzada, or nobleman, he was given the heaviest load that we could find for him, oftentimes much to the delight of the poorer coolies, as an Adamzada is exempt from coolie labour in ordinary times.

The coolies used to bolt at every opportunity, which was only natural, and there was not much difficulty in doing so. As often as not, we got into camp after dark, when the coolie simply put down his load and walked off; but as our supplies diminished, we naturally required fewer coolies--at any rate, we managed to get all our baggage into Chitral.

Moberly now handed over the company of Kashmir troops to my tender charge and departed back to Mastuj, so now I had the command of the Levies and one company added to my numerous other duties, so generally I was pretty well on the hop.

By dark the baggage had come in, the dead either buried or burnt according to their religion, and the wounded attended to and made as comfortable as we could make them under the circumstances.

Oldham and some fifty Levies who had been reconnoitring down the left bank of the river had returned, and by nine we got some dinner.

Just as we were turning in, the picket on the road over the nullah first let drive a volley, and Oldham, who was on duty, took some men and doubled out to see what was the matter. On his return, he reported the picket had heard someone moving in the nullah, and as the sentry's challenge had not been answered, they had let drive at it.

CHAPTER VIII
THE MARCH RESUMED THROUGH KILLA DRASAN

We were up by daylight the next morning, had breakfast, and were ready to march by 7 A.M. The wounded were sent back under Luard and the escort who had brought out the baggage, and we moved off in the opposite direction. Our order of march was always the same, each company taking it in turn to act as advance or rear guard, and every British officer, with the exception of Colonel Kelly and Borradaile, taking his turn on duty.

When my company of Kashmir troops was on rear or advance guard, I went with it; at other times I went with the Levies or Colonel Kelly, whichever seemed most useful.

Our march for this day led for some miles along a flat, grassy plain, a continuation of the Nisa Gol Maidan, then up and over a fairly high spur, and gradually down to the river bed opposite the village of Awi or Avi. Here we had a halt for the men to drink, as it was pretty thirsty work marching in these hot valleys. We passed a village or two on the opposite bank, but our side of the river was a desert of rocks and stones. There was a small bridge at Awi, so Cobbe, with fifty men and Shah Mirza as interpreter, was sent across to collect supplies from Buni, the village in which Jones had remained for a week after the Koragh affair. The main body continued along the right bank parallel with Cobbe's party.

During our halt two men had come in, bringing two ponies, which were much appreciated by Colonel Kelly and Borradaile.

When we got opposite Buni, there was a halt at the head of the column, and

Colonel Kelly sent me on to find out the reason.

I forgot to mention that when we were encamped at Sanoghar, a man--Chitrali--had come in, having escaped from the enemy. His brothers were followers of Suji-ul-mulk, the little boy whom Surgeon-Major Robertson, as he then was, had made Mehter, and who was besieged in Chitral with our troops. The opposition party, represented by Mahomed Issar, Sher Afzul's foster-brother, had therefore, on capturing this man, put him in quod at Killa Drasan. He had managed to escape the day of the fight, and joined us that evening, and we promptly made use of him as a guide.

This guide now informed us that the road ahead was destroyed, and would take two days to repair, but, by turning up a spur on the right, we could get past the broken part of the road.

In consequence of this there was a halt while the Levies ascended the spur and reconnoitred the top, and very soon we saw them signalling back that all was clear. Sending back the news to Colonel Kelly, I remained with the Levies, who now turned sharp to the right and began the ascent. Humayun offered me a pony, which I thankfully accepted, and noticed that there were now two or three ponies where before there had been none. I didn't say anything at the time, but shortly after there appeared an order to say all captured ponies were to be given up to the Commissariat after the battery had had first pick. It was an awful pull up that spur. I suppose we went up at least two thousand feet. I was all right, as I had a pony, but it must have been agony for the laden coolies. Once up, the going was easy enough; open, grassy downs, gradually sloping down from where we stood to the junction of the Yarkhun and Turikho valleys, though the actual sides of the tableland dropped steeply down to the rivers. By our present divergence we had turned the flank of any position the enemy could take up between Mastuj and Killa Drasan, and had also got the higher ground, our road from here onwards being down hill.

I went ahead now with the Levies, as I wanted to find out if the fort was held at Drasan.

We got to the edge of the downs by 2 P.M., looking straight down on the fort, which was the other side of the river, but from our position we could see right down into the interior.

The place was evidently deserted, for as we were watching, I saw a man go up and try the door, but, finding it closed, he went away again. The villages all round seemed deserted, and I could only see two men driving some cattle high up in the hills.

Before I had finished my sketch, the advance guard came up, and, shortly after, Colonel Kelly. There was a short halt to let the tail of the column close up, and then we commenced the descent. We were down on the river bank in twenty minutes, and the Levies waded across, I on my pony. We found the remains of a bridge which had evidently only just been destroyed, and the material, I fancy, thrown into the river. The Levies were soon up to the fort, and we had the main gate down in a jiffy by using a tree as a battering-ram, and then the Levies went through the place like professional burglars. Before I had hardly got into the courtyard they had found the grain store, and were looting it. I put Gammer Sing on sentry duty over the entrance, and, Borradaile coming up, we inspected it, and found enough grain to last us some months. We now set the Levies to work to get beams for repairing the bridge; at first we could not find any long enough, until the Levies noticed the roof poles of the verandah. We had them out and ran them down to the river bank, opposite to where the Pioneers had drawn up on the farther bank.

It took some time to build the bridge, and it was pretty rickety when done, but it saved the men having to ford. Only one man fell into the river, but he was pulled out all right. The baggage did not arrive at the bridge till dark, and most of the coolies waded across, as there was not time for them to cross in single file on the bridge. The battery also forded, but the donkeys had to be unladen and the loads carried across by hand, and the donkeys were then driven in and made to swim. It was night before the rearguard began to cross, Cobbe, who was in command, not getting in till close on nine o'clock. A couple of shots were fired after dark, and there seemed no satisfactory explanation as to why they were fired, but nobody was hit. The coolies were all put into the courtyard of the fort and a guard on the gate, and they soon had fires going, round which they huddled.

As it was impossible to carry away all the grain we had found, I got permission to issue a ration to all the coolies, who had most of them no supplies of any description, and, telling the guard who had replaced Gammer Sing to let the coolies in in single file, I then sent some Levies to drive them up like sheep. The news soon spread that food was going cheap, and they didn't require much driving. The flour was in a bin about six feet square, by four feet high, and only a small round hole at the top. We soon enlarged that so that a man could get in. I furnished him with a wooden shovel evidently meant for the job, and gave the order for the men to file in. As each man came in he received a shovelful, into his skirt tail, and then had to march round a box and out of the door. It took some two hours to finish the job, and even then the flour was not expended, while the grain, of which there was some in more bins, had not been touched. I left the guard over the door, and got back in time to get orders out for the next day's march, by which time Cobbe and the rearguard had come in, dinner was ready, and it had begun to rain.

We were camped in front of the fort, the men in a field, ourselves alongside on a praying place overlooking the river. The Levies were on the right, the ammunition and stores piled by the quarter-guard, the coolies locked up in the fort, and the pickets all right, so we turned in. Towards morning the rain began to fall heavily, so I pulled my bedding under the fort gateway, where I found Stewart and Oldham had already got the best places; however, I found a spot between two levies, and finished the night comfortably enough. We had not done a bad day's work on the whole. Marched from seven in the morning till six at night, covering some twenty miles of hilly country, made a bridge, and occupied one of the chief forts of the country. Cobbe, with the rearguard, had had the poorest time, but he had had the satisfaction of raiding into Buni.

We woke up next morning to find a dull grey sky and the rain pouring down, everything damp and miserable, and the cook having a fight with the wood to make it burn. Our proposed march for the day being only a short one, we did not start till eight A.M. As we were moving off, a Kashmir sepoy turned up who had been one of Edwardes' party, and whose life had been saved by a friendly villager who gave him some Chitrali clothes. I told him to fall in with the company, and he came down with us to Chitral. The remainder of the flour was distributed among the sepoys, and we took as much grain as we could find carriage for, but it was very little.

A small convoy of Punyal Levies joined us that day; they had been foraging up the Yarkhun valley, and had been sent after us by Moberly. Our road led along the valley through cornfields and orchards, which, in spite of the rain, looked very pretty and green. The trees were just in their first foliage and the corn about a foot high, while all the peach and apricot trees were covered with bloom. We did not see a soul on our march, but the officer in charge of the rear-guard reported that as soon as we left Killa Drasan, the villagers came hurrying down the hill in crowds.

At one place we had a short halt on account of a battery pony, which was amusing itself by rolling down a slope with a gun on its back; it was brought back nothing the worse for its escapade, and we resumed our march.

Before getting into camp, our road led up from the lower valley on to some gentle, undulating spurs of the main range of hills; here there was a cluster of villages, and every available spot was cultivated.

On one of these spurs we camped, where three small villages or clusters of houses formed a triangle, the centre of which was a cornfield. This formed an excellent halting-place, as the men were billeted in the houses, each giving the other mutual protection. We formed our mess in part of the rooms of the headman's house, one Russool of Khusht; he was foster-father to the late Nizam-ul-mulk, but had acknowledged the opposition and joined Sher Afzul. (In the photograph he is sitting half hidden behind the Mehter's left arm, with his head rather raised.)

As we had been great friends during my first visit to Chitral,--(he was awfully fond of whisky),--I've no doubt he was pleased to hear I had been his guest in his own house, but I never had an opportunity to thank him, as he left Chitral hurriedly just before our arrival. The house is the best I have seen in Chitral, a fine stone-paved courtyard, surrounded on three sides with rooms and a verandah, a fine old chinar tree near the gateway on the fourth side. The principal rooms are high and larger than usual, but of the usual pattern. I think we got two companies of the Pioneers and ourselves into this house alone.

By three o'clock we had settled down, and were getting dry. The Levies were sent out foraging, and brought in several ponies. As our stores decreased, and more ponies were brought in, we had spare ponies for riding, and we were nearly all mounted by the time we reached Chitral. However, we had not been there ten days before the owners began turning up, and we were ordered to give them back, much to our disgust. It was quite a treat to be in camp and settled before dark, and I've no doubt the coolies were as thankful as we were. The only drawback to our food was the flour of which the chupatties were made; it was coarse to a degree, and seemed to consist chiefly of minute speckly pieces of husk, which used to tickle our throats up in the most unpleasant manner, and had a nasty habit of choking the swallower, in addition to being highly indigestible. We used at last to sift the flour through linen, and the residuum was a surprise and revelation.

We had intended to march the next morning by 7 A.M., with the intention of getting to a village called Parpish, but as it was still pelting with rain, the march was deferred, to give the weather a chance of clearing up, which it very kindly did about 10 A.M., when we started. The Kashmir Company was on advance guard that day, so I went with them, two levies leading, as usual, about a quarter of a mile ahead. We struck up country for about two miles, till we got to a kotal, or saddle, from whence we had a splendid view of the surrounding country. During a halt, Colonel Kelly came up, and I was able to point out to him the different places--Koragh Defile, where Ross's party had been cut up, Reshun, where Edwardes and Fowler had held out for a week, and Barnas, a village we reached the next day. All these places were on the opposite bank of the river and several thousand feet below us. We had, by taking our present route, avoided a very difficult and dangerous part of the country, and no doubt much disgusted the inhabitants, who, on the old route, would have had all things their own way.

By two o'clock we had reached the village of Gurka, where we were met by a deputation, from whom we demanded certain supplies to be brought to our camp on pain of severe punishment if not complied with, and by 4 P.M. we got to the hamlet of Lun, and as there was a good camping ground, good water and firewood, Colonel Kelly decided to halt there. Here also supplies were demanded, the amount depending a good deal on the number of houses and the knowledge of the locality possessed by Humayun. The Lunites paid up smartly enough, as we were too close neighbours to allow of any hesitation; but the Gurka contribution had only partly come in the next morning, so that a party of the Levies was sent back, and the Gurka villagers had the trouble of bringing the loads along to Barnas, instead of only two miles into Lun, while the headman was made to carry a box of ammunition all the way to Chitral.

Before evening the sun came out, and it was very jolly in camp. We had some nice short turf to lie on, and the night was not too cold for comfort. There were good places for the pickets, and the camp was compact and handy.

CHAPTER IX
NEARING CHITRAL

The next morning, April 17th, we started sharp at 7 A.M. Two prisoners had been brought in the night before, one of whom had a Snider and twenty rounds of ammunition, the other a matchlock. They confessed that they had fought us at Nisa Gol, and stated they were now going home. We thought differently, and requested them to carry boxes of ammunition; one of them, the owner of the Snider, objected, on the ground that he was a mullah, but the objection was overruled as frivolous, and he accompanied us to Chitral. We always gave the ammunition to doubtful characters, as they were then under the direct supervision of the guard, and the loads were also more awkward and heavier than skins of flour.

We dropped down the hills now to the river bank. I was on rearguard, a nuisance at the best of times, as any check at the head of the column acts on the rearguard in increasing ratio to the length of the column, so a good deal of time is spent in wondering why the dickens they don't get on in front. That was a particularly bad day for halts: the first one was caused by the column having to cross the Perpish Gol, a very similar place to the Nisa Gol, but undefended. About two miles farther on, the road ran across the face of a cliff, and had been destroyed; it took some three hours to repair it, and then the baggage could only get along slowly.

We had some five unladen donkeys that were kept at the end of the baggage column in case of need, and, one of them trying to push past another, they both rolled over the cliff and went down about a hundred feet on to the road below, which here made a zigzag. The first donkey who came down landed on his head and broke his silly neck; but the second donkey had better luck, and landed on the first donkey in a sitting position. He got up, sniffed contemptuously at his late friend, and resumed his journey. We rolled the remains of the elect over the cliff into the river, and also resumed our course.

During this march and following ones we frequently saw the bodies of men floating down the river or stranded in shoals. They were probably the Sikhs killed with Ross, or perhaps some of Edwardes' party. By 4.30 P.M. the rearguard had crossed the cliff, and, rounding the shoulder of a spur, descended to a plain, bare of vegetation, with the exception of the inevitable wormwood. We crossed this for about a mile, and then struck down to the river, and saw the Pioneers and guns drawn up on the farther bank, and just moving off.

The road on the right hand having been again destroyed a few miles beyond, the direction of the column had been changed, and, a ford having been found, the troops had waded across, with the intention of camping that night at the village of Barnas, the rearguard arriving just in time to see the main body move off towards the village. The Levies had been left behind to help the baggage across, and rendered invaluable assistance, saving many a man from drowning.

I found most of the coolies with their loads still on the right bank of the river, leisurely proceeding to strip before wading across; the loads had to be carried on their heads, the water being well above their waists. Those loads that could be divided were carried over piecemeal, the coolie returning for the second part after taking the first across. This idea was all very fine in theory, but we found that most of the coolies, having made the first trip, sat down on the bank and proceeded to dress, leaving the remainder of their load to find its way across as best it could. Luckily Sergeant Reeves was on the farther bank, and I having also crossed over, we proceeded to drive every coolie back into the river, until there was not a load left on the opposite bank.

Rudyard Kipling, in his story of the taking of the Lungtungpen, tells how, after the scrimmage in the village, "We halted and formed up, and Liftinant Brazenose blushin' pink in the light of the mornin' sun. 'Twas the most ondacent parade I iver tuk a hand in--four-and-twenty privates an' a officer av the line in review ordher, an' not as much as wud dust a fife between 'em all in the way of clothin'." As I stood on that bank, with the evening sun lighting up the river, I thought of "Liftinant Brazenose," and also blushed. True, I was clothed myself, but instead of twenty-five, I had two hundred coolies in the same condition as that bashful officer's army.

It took us some three hours before all those loads were over, during which we had some exciting moments. Most of the coolies found the stream too strong to stem alone, and so they crossed in parties of a dozen or more, holding hands; but now and then a man would try by himself, generally with the result that half-way across he would get swept off his feet, and go floating down the stream, vainly endeavouring to regain his footing. Then there would be a rush of two or three of the levies, the man would be swung on to his feet, and his load fished for. One man I thought was bound to be drowned; he had somehow tied his load on to his head, and, being washed off his feet, his head was kept down below the water, while his legs remained waving frantically in the air. The load, being light, floated, and in this manner he was washed down stream, till two levies reached him, and, swinging him right side up, brought him spluttering ashore.

I often noticed, when sending an old man back for the remainder of his load, that some youngster who had brought his whole load across would volunteer to bring the remainder of the old man's, and, of course, I was only too glad to let him. We found the young men easy to manage, and the old men were let down lightly; it was the middle-aged man, full of strength and his own importance, who sometimes tried to raise objections, but it was getting late, and no time for fooling, so we drove our arguments home with a gun butt, and the man obeyed. The rearguard crossed in the dark, and by nine o'clock I was able to report to Colonel Kelly that everybody had arrived in camp, just as dinner was ready.

I didn't turn in till late that night, as I was on duty, and had to go scrambling round the pickets; even at that late hour I saw many men still cooking, probably preparing food for the next day.

As our supplies were now reduced to less than three days, our march the next morning was ordered for 10 A.M., in order to allow foraging parties to go out at daybreak to scoop in anything they could find.

In the meantime, I sent some levies forward to the next village to reconnoitre.

The foraging parties did not bring in much, but in our case every little was of importance, and by 10 A.M. we started. Our front in camp had been protected by a deep nullah; it took some time getting across this. By the time we cleared the village, we met our returning scouts, who reported having seen the enemy in the village of Mori, and reported their strength as some one hundred men on foot, and about twenty horsemen. So we all cheered up at the chance of a fight.

The road now dropped down to the river bed, and ran along the foot of some cliffs three or four hundred feet sheer above the roadway; there was about a mile of this, and then two miles of narrow path along the face of steep shale slopes and cliff face high above the river. Any force once caught in this place could be cut off to a man. The path was so narrow that in many places the gun ponies could not have turned round.

Colonel Kelly, however, was not to be caught in this way, so the advance guard was ordered to go right through this part of the road till they reached the maidan on the farther side, to hold that, and send back word that they had done so, the main body halting in the meantime till a clear road was announced. Half-way through, the advance guard found the road broken, but it was soon mended, and the end of the road under the cliff reached. Here there was a flattish bit of maidan for about fifty yards before the path ascended, and crossed the face of slope and cliff. The officer in command of the advance guard, thinking this was the maidan mentioned in his orders, sent back word that he was through the defile, and the road clear. Accordingly the main body advanced with a flanking picket on the cliff above. I was with Colonel Kelly at the head of the column, when, turning a corner, we came slap on top of the halted advance guard. There was no time to stop now, and the advance guard was hurried on to allow the main body to, at least, get clear of the cliffs and on the slopes. We got at last on to the slopes, but found the road broken in several places, which delayed the column considerably; luckily, I knew the Levies were on ahead, but I was glad when we reached the end of the bad track.

When we were once more on the move, I went ahead to join the Levies, and find out about the reported enemy. I found the Levies on the maidan that our advance guard should have occupied in the first place, and with them two men who had come out from the village of Mori, now only some two miles away.

These men reported that Mahomed Issar had left about 7 A.M. for Khogazi, taking all his following with him, and that he would defend a position known as the Goland Gol, just in front of that village.

I now went ahead with the Levies, and we swept through the village till we saw clear open country ahead, and satisfied ourselves that there were none of the enemy left.

I then ordered the Levies to ransack every nook and cranny for supplies, and went myself in search of a camping ground. That was not a very difficult job, and I soon came upon a nice garden and orchard, with big shady mulberry trees, and a stream flowing down the centre. On one side was the house that Mahomed Issar had occupied, and belonged to one of Sher Afzul's leading men. It was a well-built house, and inside we found some thirty sacks of caraway seeds, the stuff they put in what are called "wholesome cakes for children."

The Pioneer native officers told us that each sack was worth at least one hundred rupees in Peshawur, but we would gladly have exchanged the whole amount for half the amount of flour. One of the sacks was emptied out and the men allowed to help themselves; each man took away a handful or so, as natives are very fond of it for cooking purposes, especially for curry, a little going a long way. The whole camp smelt of caraway seed, and not an unpleasant smell either. The house was pulled down for firewood. Everyone was delighted with the camp, and it was as picturesque as could be desired. The weather was first-class for bivouacking, the trees were in full leaf, and gave a delightful shade, while the ground was covered with a good sound turf.

Foraging parties were sent out immediately, and the villagers who had met us promised to go and induce their friends to return. In fact, they did collect some ten men, each of whom brought a small sack of flour, and with that and what the foraging parties brought in, we had enough for ourselves and the coolies for three days, by which time we hoped to arrive in Chitral. A good deal of the grain brought in consisted of unhusked rice and millet, what canary birds are fed on in England,--good enough for the coolies, at any rate, most of them having been used to it from childhood. We tried to get the village water-mills going, but all the ironwork had been carried away, and we had no means of quickly refitting them, so the unthreshed rice and millet seed was issued as it was, and the men had to grind it as best they could, with stones. We still had some goats and sheep, and the men used to get a meat ration whenever there was enough to go round.

The rearguard was in by 5 P.M. that day, the first time since we had left Mastuj that it had come in before dark. Things were looking up.

The bridge at Mori had been burned, but we heard of another some two miles farther down, which, if destroyed, could be more easily mended, and as the reputed position taken up by the enemy could be turned from the right bank of the river, it was determined to repair it.

Consequently, early the next morning, Oldham and his Sappers, with a covering party of one company of Pioneers under Bethune, and the Hunza Levies, started to repair the bridge, and be ready to cross and turn the enemy's flank, should he be found awaiting us.

An hour later the main body started over a road leading along a high cliff. Here and there the enemy had evidently made attempts to destroy the road, but so ineffectually that the advance guard hardly delayed its advance for five minutes to repair it, and by 10 A.M. we had reached the broken bridge, and found Oldham and his party hard at work mending it.

The great difficulty was want of beams to stretch across from pier to pier, but attempts were being made to get these from an adjacent village on the opposite bank of the river.

The bridge would not be ready for some two hours at earliest, so Colonel Kelly sent me on to reconnoitre the Goland Gol, which we expected the enemy to hold. I kicked my pony into a gallop and hurried forward.

About a quarter of a mile farther on, I saw one of the road-bearing beams of the destroyed bridge which had stranded on the opposite bank, and sent back a note describing where it could be found.

Another quarter of a mile brought me up to the Punyal Levies, who were already reconnoitring the spurs where the army were supposed to be; but after a careful look through my glasses, we came to the conclusion that there was no enemy, and again advanced. We reached the Goland Gol, which is a narrow nullah running up into the hills on the left bank of the river, the sides being impracticable for several miles, and down the centre of which rushes a mountain torrent, the road to Chitral crossing this latter, just before it flows into the Yarkhun river, by means of a bridge. This bridge we found destroyed, but I sent half the Levies across by fording the stream a hundred yards higher up, and made them occupy the ridge on the far side, and put the remainder on to repair the bridge. I also gave my pony and a note to one of the levies, whom I sent back with a report to Colonel Kelly, who, on receiving it, had work on the other bridge knocked off, as it was no longer wanted.

We hunted for the beams of the Goland Gol bridge, which we found jammed in the stream a short way down, only one out of the four being smashed, and soon had them back in their places. Then we laid a roadway of boards from a hut near, and filled up the holes with branches, and had the bridge ready before the advance guard arrived. I sent back word, and then crossed the stream and joined the remainder of the Levies on the farther side. Here I found several sangars which covered the approaches to the bridge, and soon had them down, and then went on to the village of Khogazi, which was about a mile ahead.

We swept through that village in the usual manner from end to end, finding only one man who turned out to be a Gilgiti; he had been carried into slavery several years previously, but had married and settled down. From him we learned that Mohamed Issar, with a following of about one hundred men, had arrived the day before about noon; shortly after, a messenger came in from Sher Afzul, telling him to come into Chitral without delay, and consequently the whole party had set off about 4 P.M. All the villagers, he said, had fled up the Goland Gol to the higher hills, but he would try and bring in any he could find. He did not think the enemy would try and fight again, though there was a place called Baitali, just before the opening into the Chitral valley, where, if any opposition was offered, it would be made. The position could be turned from both flanks, and ponies could go, but it was not a good road. He professed himself as willing to go and find out if the Baitali Pari was occupied, so I sent him off. I knew the place as one of the worst bits in the whole road between Mastuj and Chitral, but I also knew it could be passed by crossing the river at Khogazi and climbing the hills on the right hand, and down on to the Chitral river above its junction with the Yarkhun river. This would be convenient if the Chitral bridge was destroyed, as it would take us along the right bank, on which stands the fort; but I knew also of a ford about two miles above the Chitral bridge, where we could cover our passage, as the ground was level and open.

CHAPTER X
WE REACH THE GOAL

I picked out a camping ground even better than we had enjoyed at Mori, and then shared some chupatties and chocolate with Rajah Akbar Khan.

The main body came in by two o'clock, and the baggage shortly after. Foraging parties were sent out, and Oldham sent to report on the bridge in case we decided to cross. He reported it as practicable, so a guard was put on it to keep it so.

Stewart came into camp that day like a bear with a sore head. "Here had he been hauling his guns over condemned precipices in pursuit of an invisible enemy. Call this war! it was only a route march. For a promenade he preferred the Empire Theatre."

We tried to console him with hopes of a fight before Chitral, but he declared the Chitralis had grievously disappointed him, and went off to see about fodder for his ponies. Alas, poor Stewart! he didn't get his desire.

As soon as we had settled down in camp, Colonel Kelly told me to try and find some man who would carry a letter into Chitral, to warn the garrison of our approach. I got hold of Shah Mirza, and asked him if he knew anyone who would go. First, we tried the man who had escaped from Killa Drasan, but he refused; then Shah Mirza volunteered to go himself, but he was too useful to be spared. Just as we were wondering who we could get to go, Humayun and Akbar Khan turned up, evidently excited, and escorting a man who was bearing letters from Chitral. He handed over a letter addressed to "The officer commanding troops advancing from Gilgit." Inside was a letter from Surgeon-Major Robertson, saying that Sher Afzul had fled on the night of the 18th April, and the siege of Chitral was raised. He enclosed a return of the killed and wounded, which, he requested, might be forwarded to India. Then we went through the list, and came across poor Baird's name among the killed. This was the first we had heard of it, the natives all declaring that it was Gurdon who had been killed. Among the wounded we came across Surgeon-Major Robertson severely and Captain Campbell severely. Poor old General Baj Singh and Major Bicham Singh were killed, and all together the casualties amounted to one hundred and four killed and wounded out of three hundred and seventy combatants. So the garrison had evidently had a lively time of it. Then we set to work and pumped the messenger dry of all the news he could tell, the details of which are now too well known for me to relate. The man had a passport from Surgeon-Major Robertson, sending him to Killa Drasan, so he was allowed to go. We also found out from him that there was no enemy between us and Chitral, at which Stewart swore openly. My spy returned on meeting the Chitral messenger.

There was no difficulty now in getting a man to go to Chitral, so we sent off one with a note, saying we should arrive next day by noon, the 20th April.

The news had spread quickly through camp, and the native officers came round to hear about it. We sent back a post to Mastuj by some Nagar Levies who had just brought in a post, and then had a good discussion as to the causes that led to the raising of the siege.

I don't know if any of the other officers felt it, but I know, speaking for myself, that with the departure of any uncertainty about our arrival in Chitral in time to save the garrison, a good deal of interest also departed.

I felt inclined to agree with Stewart, that the enemy had given us a just cause for complaint by not playing the game. At any rate, they might have given us a run for our money in front of Chitral, and this seemed to be the general idea throughout the column, consequently our opinion of the Chitrali pluck sank considerably.

We marched at 6 A.M. the next morning punctually, and by noon the advance guard was in the Chitral valley. A halt was ordered to allow the main body to form up, as the guns had had a bad time getting through the Baitali Pari, and had to be unloaded and carried by hand for some distance.

After about two miles we came in sight of the Chitral bridge, which had not been destroyed, and, soon after, of the fort, with the Union Jack still floating on one of the towers.

We crossed the bridge, closed up the column on the other side, the buglers were sent to the front, and we marched on to the fort with as much swagger as we could put on.

We found the garrison in front of the main gate, and were very glad to shake hands again with all our old friends and congratulate them on their splendid defence.

We had a short halt, and then moved on, and took up a position covering the fort, with our front on a nullah and pickets facing south. Our bivouac was in a nice shady garden, with plenty of good water and wood.

When the men had settled down in camp, the officers went back to the fort, where the garrison gave us breakfast, or rather lunch. There was a great deal to hear and tell, and for the first time we began to realise what a touch-and-go time the garrison had been having. There was only one pause in the conversation, and good old Stewart chipped in with "D'ye think, now, there's any chance of another fight?"

After tiffin, we went round and saw all the sights of interest, and generally interviewed the lions. We saw Harley's mine, the gun tower, the enemy's sangars, the hospital, and we did not forget poor Baird's grave, which was just outside the main gate. Then we went back to camp, and most of us took the opportunity to write home. I also took a photograph when everyone was assembled over the homely cup of tea. The bottles on the table look like whisky, but they only contain treacle made by melting down country goor, the extract of sugar-cane. It was our substitute for butter or jam, luxuries we had not seen for weeks. Whisky was a dream of the past, and rum a scarcity. In fact, there was no difference between what we and the sepoys ate, except in the manner of cooking.

We went to sleep that night with the blissful consciousness that the next day was a halt at any rate, and I think we needed the rest. We had put on our least ragged coats to march in and make as brave a show as possible, but our kit generally was in a pretty disreputable state, and there was a good deal of work wanted in the laundry line. Most of us, also, had misgivings about our boots. I was reduced to choosing between boots with large holes in the soles or chuplies mended with string; the boots I kept for show days, as the holes didn't show, and the chuplies for ordinary work. Most of the other officers were much in the same plight.

So ended the march of Colonel Kelly's column to Chitral. Our record, on the whole, was not bad, though, of course, judging by actual distance, we had not done much; it was more the difficult nature of the ground and the altitude at which some of it was done that lent interest to the march, and I am unfeignedly glad my luck caused me to participate in it.

The next day the Kashmir troops of the garrison came out and camped with us, and revelled in the fresh air after the poisonous atmosphere of the fort. Poor chaps! they were walking skeletons, bloodless, and as quiet as the ghosts they resembled, most of them reduced to jerseys and garments of any description, but still plucky and of good heart. They cheered up wonderfully in a few days with good fresh air and sleep, and marched from Chitral quite briskly when they left.

The next day I again went round the fort and got some photos, which follow. One of the British officers of the garrison beneath the gun tower, which was set on fire, and during the extinguishing of which Surgeon-Major Robertson, the British agent, was wounded by a Snider bullet. There is also the loophole, afterwards made, from which a sentry inside the tower could fire at anyone within a few feet. Then I got Harley to show me the site of his sortie, and pretty grisly the place looked, but unfortunately the photograph I took, showing the mine lying open like a ditch to the foot of the tower, was a "wrong un." But I succeeded in getting one showing the mouth of the mine, with the excavated earth.

Then I took one of the sangars from the interior, with the little shelters used by the Pathans when not amusing themselves with rifle practice. The water tower is just visible through the foliage.

Then I took a photo of the fort from the corner by the gun tower looking towards the musjid, which is shown in a photo at the beginning of the book, but taken in more peaceful times. It shows the bridge in the distance, which the fire of the Sikhs made too hot for the Chitralis, who had to cross over the hills in the daytime.

Then I took Harley and the two native officers of the 14th Sikhs, Subadar Gurmuskh Singh and Jemadar Atta Singh. Atta Singh put on white gloves to grace the occasion, but evidently trembled violently during the exposure.

I got a shot at Borradaile sitting in a shelter Oldham had run up for himself; the hawk and spear were looted at Sanoghar, I think. Borradaile looks very like Diogenes in his tub. I also took some Kafirs who strolled into camp. We used to buy their daggers, but they got to asking as much as twenty rupees for a good one after a time. Every Kaffir has a dagger, some of them very good ones, but roughly finished.

After we had been some days in Chitral, some of the 3rd Brigade under General Gatacre arrived, followed by General Low and the headquarter staff.

There was a parade of all the troops in Chitral, with the usual tomasha of salutes and inspection. We were then formed up in a square, and General Low made a speech, in which he said that the honour of raising the siege of Chitral belonged to Colonel Kelly's force; whereat we of that force threw out our chest and patted ourselves on the back. We also winked the other eye.

Little Suji-ul-mulk, the Mehter elect, was present at the review with his following, and personally conducted by the B.A., resplendent in political uniform, we soldiers being in khaki. The parade was dismissed, and, headed by the pipes of the general's escort and of the 4th Gurkhas, we marched back to our camp.

A few days afterwards, I was ordered back to Gilgit, to take up Baird's duties, and the Pioneers followed shortly after.

The Kashmir troops have gone back to Sudin on relief, and the Pioneers have followed. There are only one or two of us now left in Gilgit who took part in the march; but, black or white, it is a bond between us which will, I hope, last our lifetime.

www.bookjungle.com email: sales@bookjungle.com fax: 630-214-0564 mail: Book Jungle PO Box 2226 Champaign, IL 61825

The Codes Of Hammurabi And Moses
W. W. Davies

QTY

The discovery of the Hammurabi Code is one of the greatest achievements of archaeology, and is of paramount interest, not only to the student of the Bible, but also to all those interested in ancient history...

Religion   ISBN: *1-59462-338-4*   Pages:132
MSRP $12.95

The Theory of Moral Sentiments
Adam Smith

QTY

This work from 1749. contains original theories of conscience amd moral judgment and it is the foundation for systemof morals.

Philosophy   ISBN: *1-59462-777-0*   Pages:536
MSRP $19.95

Jessica's First Prayer
Hesba Stretton

QTY

In a screened and secluded corner of one of the many railway-bridges which span the streets of London there could be seen a few years ago, from five o'clock every morning until half past eight, a tidily set-out coffee-stall, consisting of a trestle and board, upon which stood two large tin cans, with a small fire of charcoal burning under each so as to keep the coffee boiling during the early hours of the morning when the work-people were thronging into the city on their way to their daily toil...

Pages:84

Childrens   ISBN: *1-59462-373-2*   *MSRP $9.95*

My Life and Work
Henry Ford

QTY

Henry Ford revolutionized the world with his implementation of mass production for the Model T automobile. Gain valuable business insight into his life and work with his own auto-biography... "We have only started on our development of our country we have not as yet, with all our talk of wonderful progress, done more than scratch the surface. The progress has been wonderful enough but..."

Pages:300

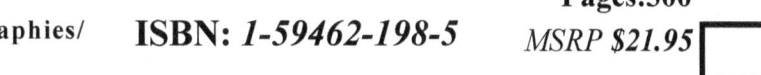

Biographies/   ISBN: *1-59462-198-5*   *MSRP $21.95*

www.bookjungle.com *email: sales@bookjungle.com fax: 630-214-0564 mail: Book Jungle PO Box 2226 Champaign, IL 61825*

The Art of Cross-Examination
Francis Wellman

QTY

I presume it is the experience of every author, after his first book is published upon an important subject, to be almost overwhelmed with a wealth of ideas and illustrations which could readily have been included in his book, and which to his own mind, at least, seem to make a second edition inevitable. Such certainly was the case with me; and when the first edition had reached its sixth impression in five months, I rejoiced to learn that it seemed to my publishers that the book had met with a sufficiently favorable reception to justify a second and considerably enlarged edition. ..

Pages:412

Reference   ISBN: *1-59462-647-2*   *MSRP $19.95*

On the Duty of Civil Disobedience
Henry David Thoreau

QTY

Thoreau wrote his famous essay, On the Duty of Civil Disobedience, as a protest against an unjust but popular war and the immoral but popular institution of slave-owning. He did more than write—he declined to pay his taxes, and was hauled off to gaol in consequence. Who can say how much this refusal of his hastened the end of the war and of slavery ?

Law   ISBN: *1-59462-747-9*   **Pages:48**
MSRP $7.45

Dream Psychology Psychoanalysis for Beginners
Sigmund Freud

QTY

Sigmund Freud, born Sigismund Schlomo Freud (May 6, 1856 - September 23, 1939), was a Jewish-Austrian neurologist and psychiatrist who co-founded the psychoanalytic school of psychology. Freud is best known for his theories of the unconscious mind, especially involving the mechanism of repression; his redefinition of sexual desire as mobile and directed towards a wide variety of objects; and his therapeutic techniques, especially his understanding of transference in the therapeutic relationship and the presumed value of dreams as sources of insight into unconscious desires.

Pages:196

Psychology   ISBN: *1-59462-905-6*   *MSRP $15.45*

The Miracle of Right Thought
Orison Swett Marden

QTY

Believe with all of your heart that you will do what you were made to do. When the mind has once formed the habit of holding cheerful, happy, prosperous pictures, it will not be easy to form the opposite habit. It does not matter how improbable or how far away this realization may see, or how dark the prospects may be, if we visualize them as best we can, as vividly as possible, hold tenaciously to them and vigorously struggle to attain them, they will gradually become actualized, realized in the life. But a desire, a longing without endeavor, a yearning abandoned or held indifferently will vanish without realization.

Pages:360

Self Help   ISBN: *1-59462-644-8*   *MSRP $25.45*

www.bookjungle.com email: sales@bookjungle.com fax: 630-214-0564 mail: Book Jungle PO Box 2226 Champaign, IL 61825

QTY

	Title	ISBN	Price
☐	**The Rosicrucian Cosmo-Conception Mystic Christianity** by *Max Heindel*	ISBN: *1-59462-188-8*	**$38.95**
	The Rosicrucian Cosmo-conception is not dogmatic, neither does it appeal to any other authority than the reason of the student. It is: not controversial, but is: sent forth in the, hope that it may help to clear...		New Age/Religion Pages 646
☐	**Abandonment To Divine Providence** by *Jean-Pierre de Caussade*	ISBN: *1-59462-228-0*	**$25.95**
	"The Rev. Jean Pierre de Caussade was one of the most remarkable spiritual writers of the Society of Jesus in France in the 18th Century. His death took place at Toulouse in 1751. His works have gone through many editions and have been republished...		Inspirational/Religion Pages 400
☐	**Mental Chemistry** by *Charles Haanel*	ISBN: *1-59462-192-6*	**$23.95**
	Mental Chemistry allows the change of material conditions by combining and appropriately utilizing the power of the mind. Much like applied chemistry creates something new and unique out of careful combinations of chemicals the mastery of mental chemistry...		New Age Pages 354
☐	**The Letters of Robert Browning and Elizabeth Barret Barrett 1845-1846 vol II** by *Robert Browning and Elizabeth Barrett*	ISBN: *1-59462-193-4*	**$35.95**
			Biographies Pages 596
☐	**Gleanings In Genesis (volume I)** by *Arthur W. Pink*	ISBN: *1-59462-130-6*	**$27.45**
	Appropriately has Genesis been termed "the seed plot of the Bible" for in it we have, in germ form, almost all of the great doctrines which are afterwards fully developed in the books of Scripture which follow...		Religion/Inspirational Pages 420
☐	**The Master Key** by *L. W. de Laurence*	ISBN: *1-59462-001-6*	**$30.95**
	In no branch of human knowledge has there been a more lively increase of the spirit of research during the past few years than in the study of Psychology, Concentration and Mental Discipline. The requests for authentic lessons in Thought Control, Mental Discipline and...		New Age/Business Pages 422
☐	**The Lesser Key Of Solomon Goetia** by *L. W. de Laurence*	ISBN: *1-59462-092-X*	**$9.95**
	This translation of the first book of the "Lernegton" which is now for the first time made accessible to students of Talismanic Magic was done, after careful collation and edition, from numerous Ancient Manuscripts in Hebrew, Latin, and French...		New Age/Occult Pages 92
☐	**Rubaiyat Of Omar Khayyam** by *Edward Fitzgerald*	ISBN:*1-59462-332-5*	**$13.95**
	Edward Fitzgerald, whom the world has already learned, in spite of his own efforts to remain within the shadow of anonymity, to look upon as one of the rarest poets of the century, was born at Bredfield, in Suffolk, on the 31st of March, 1809. He was the third son of John Purcell...		Music Pages 172
☐	**Ancient Law** by *Henry Maine*	ISBN: *1-59462-128-4*	**$29.95**
	The chief object of the following pages is to indicate some of the earliest ideas of mankind, as they are reflected in Ancient Law, and to point out the relation of those ideas to modern thought.		Religiom/History Pages 452
☐	**Far-Away Stories** by *William J. Locke*	ISBN: *1-59462-129-2*	**$19.45**
	"Good wine needs no bush, but a collection of mixed vintages does. And this book is just such a collection. Some of the stories I do not want to remain buried for ever in the museum files of dead magazine-numbers an author's not unpardonable vanity..."		Fiction Pages 272
☐	**Life of David Crockett** by *David Crockett*	ISBN: *1-59462-250-7*	**$27.45**
	"Colonel David Crockett was one of the most remarkable men of the times in which he lived. Born in humble life, but gifted with a strong will, an indomitable courage, and unremitting perseverance...		Biographies/New Age Pages 424
☐	**Lip-Reading** by *Edward Nitchie*	ISBN: *1-59462-206-X*	**$25.95**
	Edward B. Nitchie, founder of the New York School for the Hard of Hearing, now the Nitchie School of Lip-Reading, Inc, wrote "LIP-READING Principles and Practice". The development and perfecting of this meritorious work on lip-reading was an undertaking...		How-to Pages 400
☐	**A Handbook of Suggestive Therapeutics, Applied Hypnotism, Psychic Science** by *Henry Munro*	ISBN: *1-59462-214-0*	**$24.95**
			Health/New Age/Health/Self-help Pages 376
☐	**A Doll's House: and Two Other Plays** by *Henrik Ibsen*	ISBN: *1-59462-112-8*	**$19.95**
	Henrik Ibsen created this classic when in revolutionary 1848 Rome. Introducing some striking concepts in playwriting for the realist genre, this play has been studied the world over.		Fiction/Classics/Plays 308
☐	**The Light of Asia** by *sir Edwin Arnold*	ISBN: *1-59462-204-3*	**$13.95**
	In this poetic masterpiece, Edwin Arnold describes the life and teachings of Buddha. The man who was to become known as Buddha to the world was born as Prince Gautama of India but he rejected the worldly riches and abandoned the reigns of power when...		Religion/History/Biographies Pages 170
☐	**The Complete Works of Guy de Maupassant** by *Guy de Maupassant*	ISBN: *1-59462-157-8*	**$16.95**
	"For days and days, nights and nights, I had dreamed of that first kiss which was to consecrate our engagement, and I knew not on what spot I should put my lips..."		Fiction/Classics Pages 240
☐	**The Art of Cross-Examination** by *Francis L. Wellman*	ISBN: *1-59462-309-0*	**$26.95**
	Written by a renowned trial lawyer, Wellman imparts his experience and uses case studies to explain how to use psychology to extract desired information through questioning.		How-to/Science/Reference Pages 408
☐	**Answered or Unanswered?** by *Louisa Vaughan*	ISBN: *1-59462-248-5*	**$10.95**
	Miracles of Faith in China		Religion Pages 112
☐	**The Edinburgh Lectures on Mental Science (1909)** by *Thomas*	ISBN: *1-59462-008-3*	**$11.95**
	This book contains the substance of a course of lectures recently given by the writer in the Queen Street Hall, Edinburgh. Its purpose is to indicate the Natural Principles governing the relation between Mental Action and Material Conditions...		New Age/Psychology Pages 148
☐	**Ayesha** by *H. Rider Haggard*	ISBN: *1-59462-301-5*	**$24.95**
	Verily and indeed it is the unexpected that happens! Probably if there was one person upon the earth from whom the Editor of this, and of a certain previous history, did not expect to hear again...		Classics Pages 380
☐	**Ayala's Angel** by *Anthony Trollope*	ISBN: *1-59462-352-X*	**$29.95**
	The two girls were both pretty, but Lucy who was twenty-one who supposed to be simple and comparatively unattractive, whereas Ayala was credited, as her Bombwhat romantic name might show, with poetic charm and a taste for romance. Ayala when her father died was nineteen...		Fiction Pages 484
☐	**The American Commonwealth** by *James Bryce*	ISBN: *1-59462-286-8*	**$34.45**
	An interpretation of American democratic political theory. It examines political mechanics and society from the perspective of Scotsman James Bryce		Politics Pages 572
☐	**Stories of the Pilgrims** by *Margaret P. Pumphrey*	ISBN: *1-59462-116-0*	**$17.95**
	This book explores pilgrims religious oppression in England as well as their escape to Holland and eventual crossing to America on the Mayflower, and their early days in New England...		History Pages 268

www.bookjungle.com email: sales@bookjungle.com fax: 630-214-0564 mail: Book Jungle PO Box 2226 Champaign, IL 61825

			QTY

The Fasting Cure by *Sinclair Upton* ISBN: *1-59462-222-1* **$13.95**
In the Cosmopolitan Magazine for May, 1910, and in the Contemporary Review (London) for April, 1910, I published an article dealing with my experiences in fasting. I have written a great many magazine articles, but never one which attracted so much attention... New Age/Self Help/Health Pages 164

Hebrew Astrology by *Sepharial* ISBN: *1-59462-308-2* **$13.45**
In these days of advanced thinking it is a matter of common observation that we have left many of the old landmarks behind and that we are now pressing forward to greater heights and to a wider horizon than that which represented the mind-content of our progenitors... Astrology Pages 144

Thought Vibration or The Law of Attraction in the Thought World ISBN: *1-59462-127-6* **$12.95**
by *William Walker Atkinson* Psychology/Religion Pages 144

Optimism by *Helen Keller* ISBN: *1-59462-108-X* **$15.95**
Helen Keller was blind, deaf, and mute since 19 months old, yet famously learned how to overcome these handicaps, communicate with the world, and spread her lectures promoting optimism. An inspiring read for everyone... Biographies/Inspirational Pages 84

Sara Crewe by *Frances Burnett* ISBN: *1-59462-360-0* **$9.45**
In the first place, Miss Minchin lived in London. Her home was a large, dull, tall one, in a large, dull square, where all the houses were alike, and all the sparrows were alike, and where all the door-knockers made the same heavy sound... Childrens/Classic Pages 88

The Autobiography of Benjamin Franklin by *Benjamin Franklin* ISBN: *1-59462-135-7* **$24.95**
The Autobiography of Benjamin Franklin has probably been more extensively read than any other American historical work, and no other book of its kind has had such ups and downs of fortune. Franklin lived for many years in England, where he was agent... Biographies/History Pages 332

Name	
Email	
Telephone	
Address	
City, State ZIP	

☐ Credit Card   ☐ Check / Money Order

Credit Card Number	
Expiration Date	
Signature	

Please Mail to: Book Jungle
PO Box 2226
Champaign, IL 61825
or Fax to: 630-214-0564

ORDERING INFORMATION

web: *www.bookjungle.com*
email: *sales@bookjungle.com*
fax: *630-214-0564*
mail: *Book Jungle PO Box 2226 Champaign, IL 61825*
or PayPal *to sales@bookjungle.com*

Please contact us for bulk discounts

DIRECT-ORDER TERMS

20% Discount if You Order Two or More Books
Free Domestic Shipping!
Accepted: Master Card, Visa, Discover, American Express

www.ingramcontent.com/pod-product-compliance
Lightning Source LLC
Chambersburg PA
CBHW081326040426
42453CB00013B/2314